GRAPHIC HISTORY

THE ADVENTURES OF MARCO POLO

by Roger Smalley

illustrated by Brian Bascle

Consultant:
Margaretta S. Handke, PhD
Professor of World History
Minnesota State University, Mankato

Capstone press
Mankato, Minnesota

Graphic Library books are published by Capstone Press,
151 Good Counsel Drive, P.O. Box 669, Mankato, Minnesota 56002.
www.capstonepress.com

Printed in the United States of America

1 2 3 4 5 6 10 09 08 07 06 05

Library of Congress Cataloging-in-Publication Data
Smalley, Roger.
The adventures of Marco Polo / by Roger Smalley; illustrated by Brian Bascle.
p. cm.—(Graphic library. Graphic history)
Includes bibliographical references and index.
ISBN 0-7368-3830-9 (hardcover)
ISBN 0-7368-5240-9 (paperback)
1. Polo, Marco, 1254–1323?—Travel—Juvenile literature. 2. Explorers—Italy—Biography—Juvenile literature. 3. Travel, Medieval—Juvenile literature. 4. Asia—Description and travel—Juvenile literature. I. Bascle, Brian, ill. II. Title. III. Series.
G370.P9S64 2005
910.4—dc22 2004015498

Summary: The story of Marco Polo's journey to China, describing some of the things he saw while in the service of Kublai Khan.

Editor's note: Direct quotations from primary sources are indicated by a yellow background.

Direct quotations appear on the following pages:
Pages 14, 18, 19, 20, 21, from *The Travels of Marco Polo* by Marco Polo; translated by Ronald Latham (New York: Penguin Books, 1988).

Credits
Art Director and Storyboard Artist
Jason Knudson

Art Director
Heather Kindseth

Editor
Blake A. Hoena

Acknowledgment
Capstone Press thanks Philip Charles Crawford, Library Director, Essex High School, Essex, Vermont, and columnist for *Knowledge Quest*, for his assistance in the preparation of this book.

TABLE OF CONTENTS

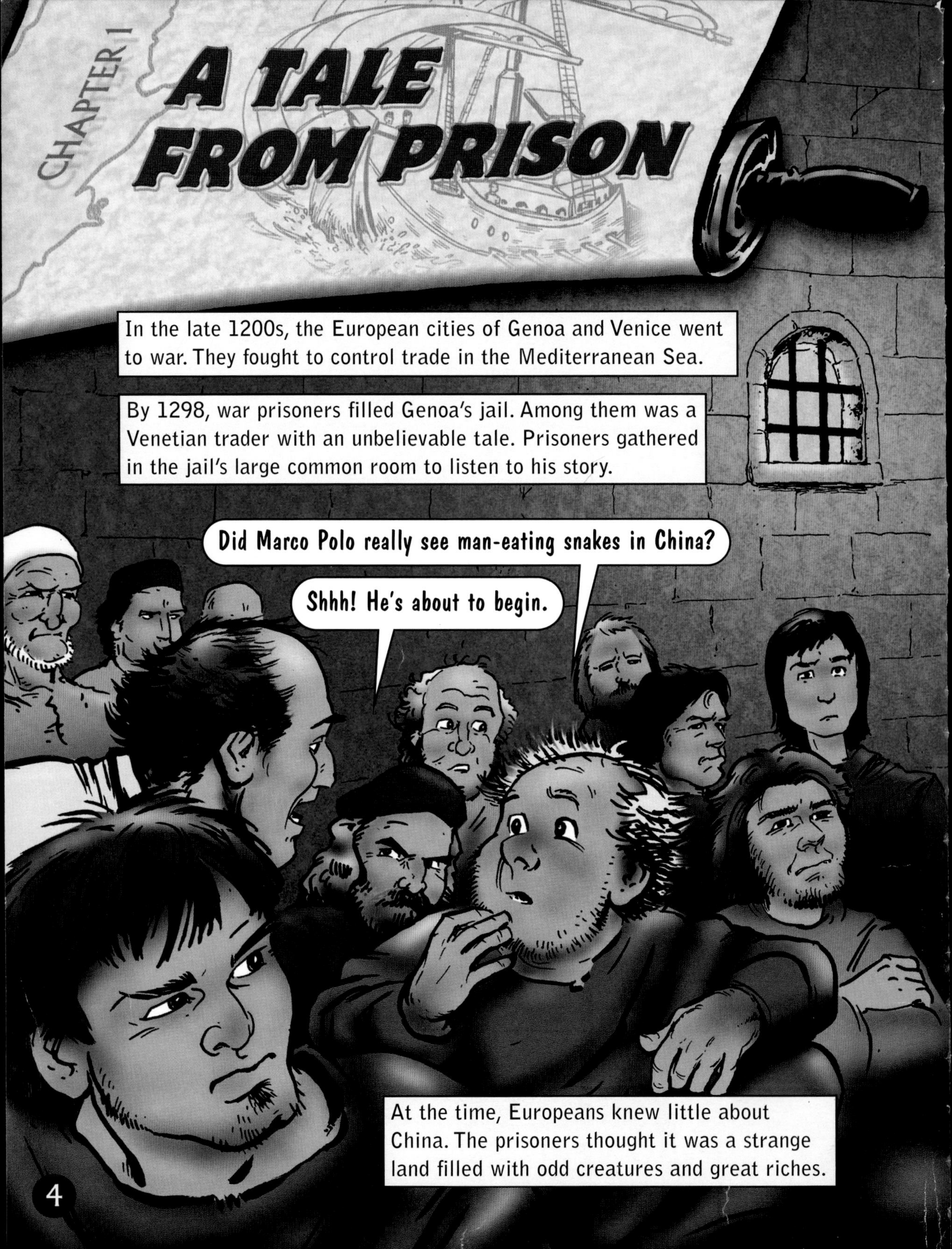
CHAPTER 1
A TALE FROM PRISON
In the late 1200s, the European cities of Genoa and Venice went to war. They fought to control trade in the Mediterranean Sea.
By 1298, war prisoners filled Genoa's jail. Among them was a Venetian trader with an unbelievable tale. Prisoners gathered in the jail's large common room to listen to his story.
Did Marco Polo really see man-eating snakes in China?
Shhh! He's about to begin.
At the time, Europeans knew little about China. The prisoners thought it was a strange land filled with odd creatures and great riches.

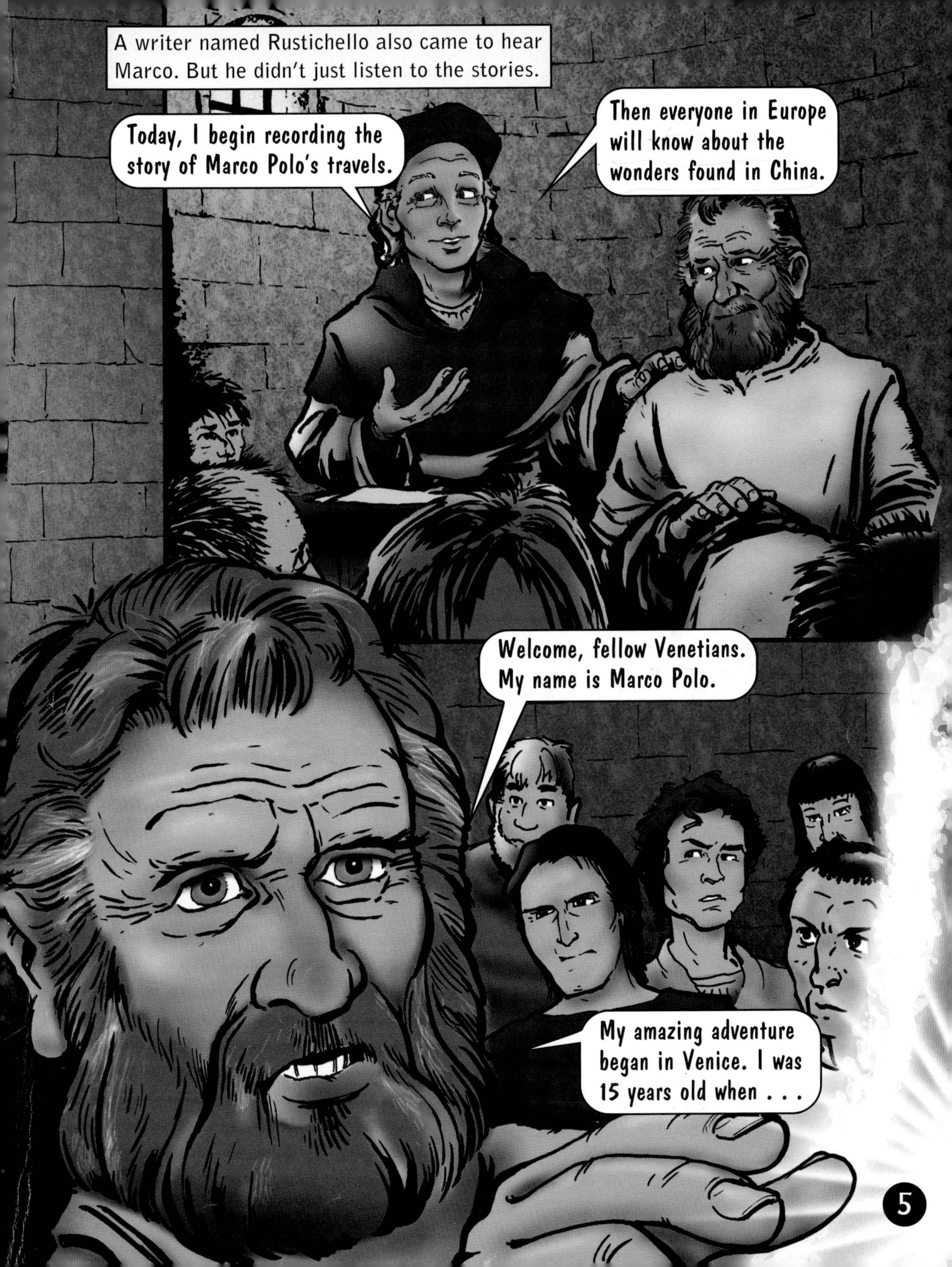

A writer named Rustichello also came to hear Marco. But he didn't just listen to the stories.
Today, I begin recording the story of Marco Polo's travels.
Then everyone in Europe will know about the wonders found in China.
Welcome, fellow Venetians. My name is Marco Polo.
My amazing adventure began in Venice. I was 15 years old when . . .

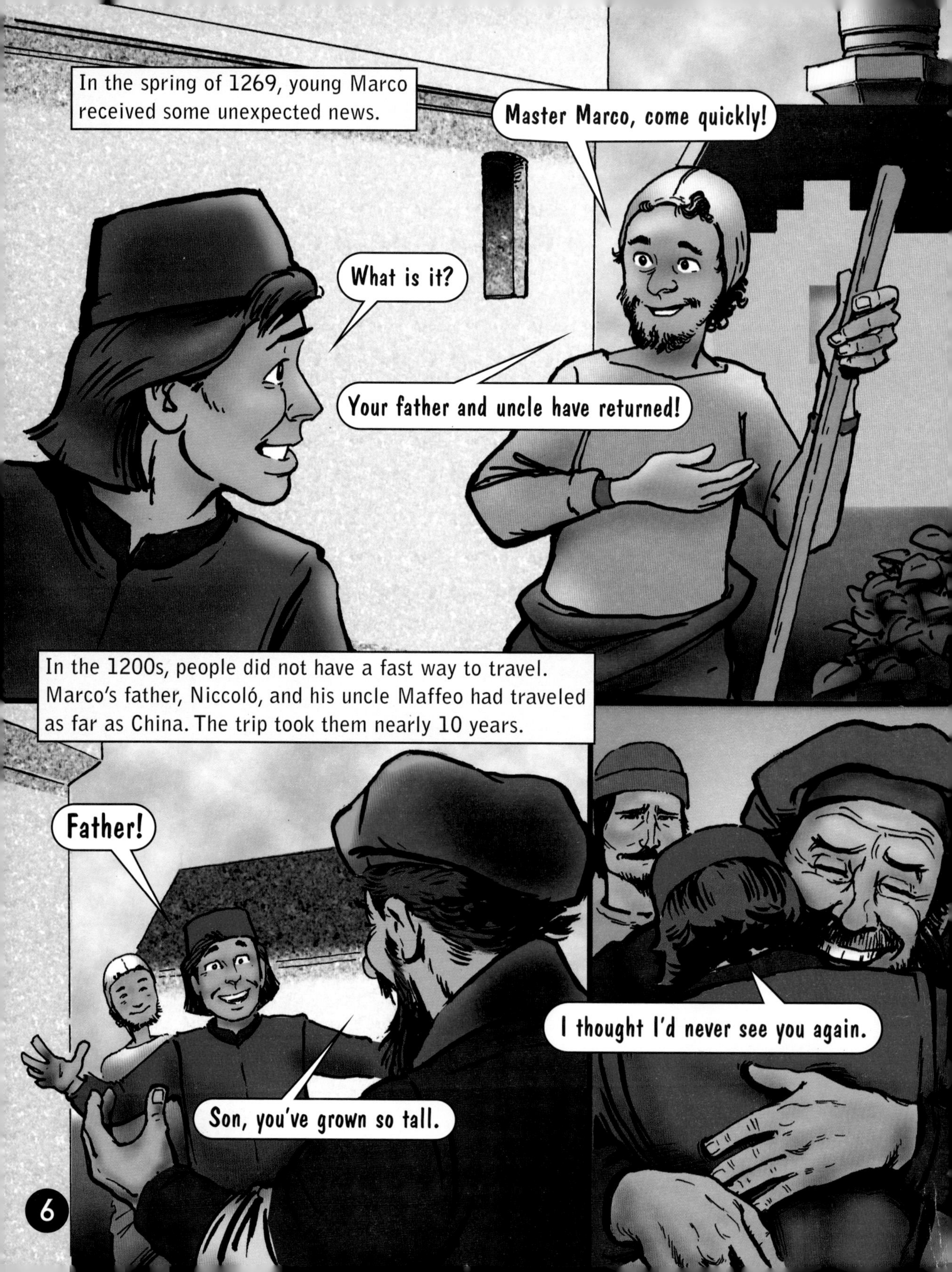
In the spring of 1269, young Marco received some unexpected news.
Master Marco, come quickly!
What is it?
Your father and uncle have returned!
In the 1200s, people did not have a fast way to travel. Marco's father, Niccoló, and his uncle Maffeo had traveled as far as China. The trip took them nearly 10 years.
Father!
Son, you've grown so tall.
I thought I'd never see you again.

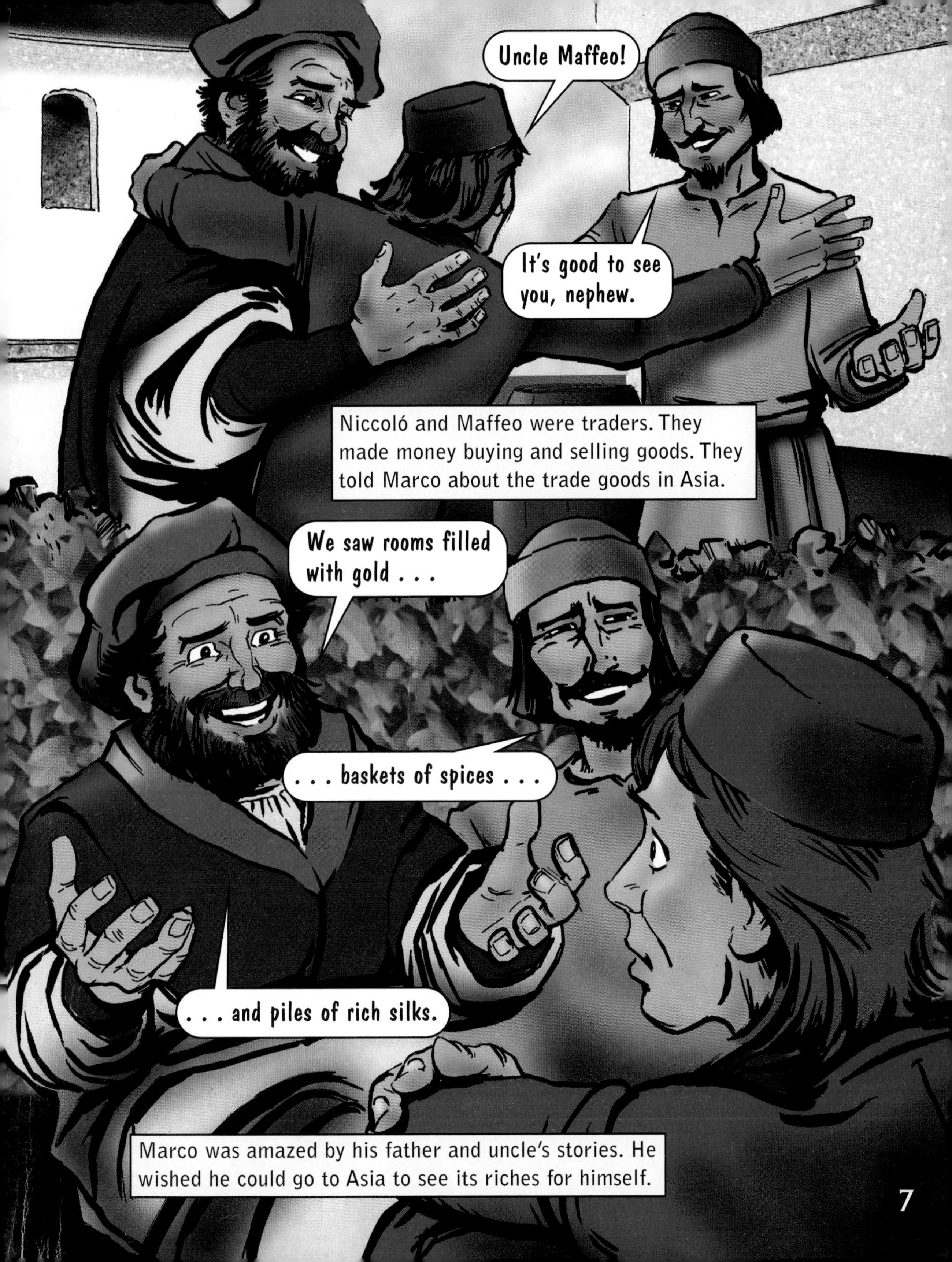

Uncle Maffeo!
It's good to see you, nephew.
Niccoló and Maffeo were traders. They made money buying and selling goods. They told Marco about the trade goods in Asia.
We saw rooms filled with gold . . .
. . . baskets of spices . . .
. . . and piles of rich silks.
Marco was amazed by his father and uncle's stories. He wished he could go to Asia to see its riches for himself.

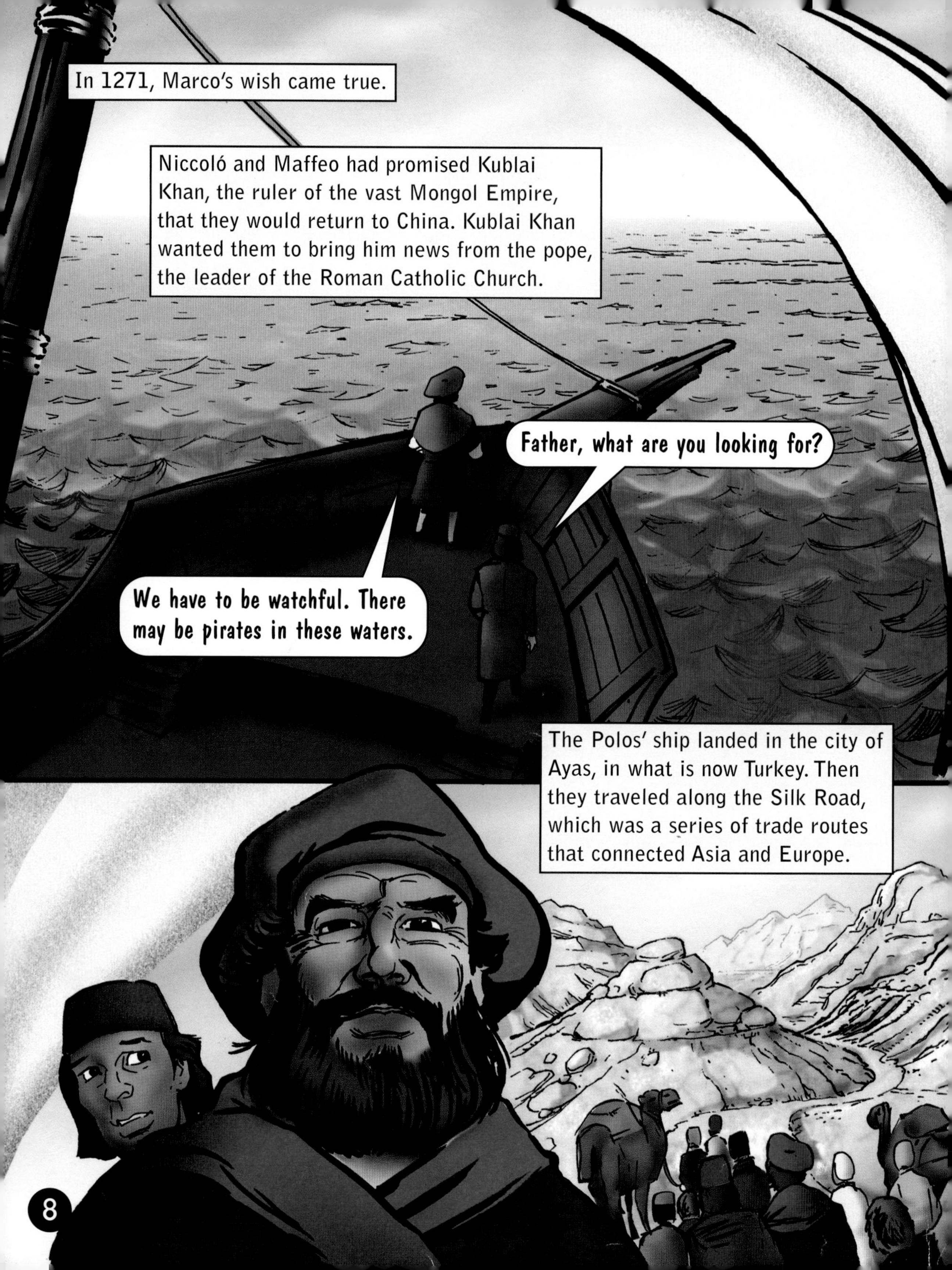
In 1271, Marco's wish came true.
Niccoló and Maffeo had promised Kublai Khan, the ruler of the vast Mongol Empire, that they would return to China. Kublai Khan wanted them to bring him news from the pope, the leader of the Roman Catholic Church.
Father, what are you looking for?
We have to be watchful. There may be pirates in these waters.
The Polos' ship landed in the city of Ayas, in what is now Turkey. Then they traveled along the Silk Road, which was a series of trade routes that connected Asia and Europe.

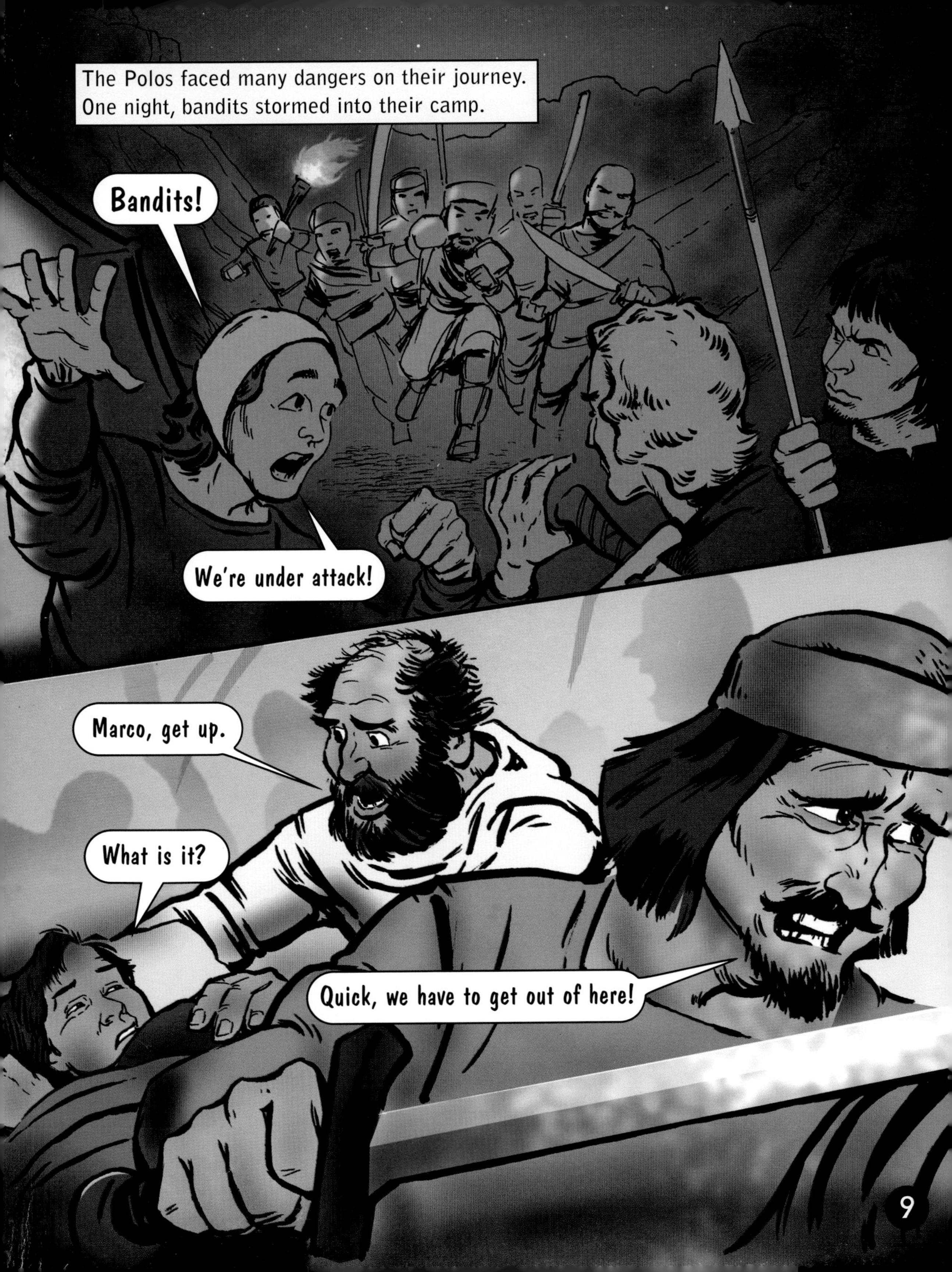
The Polos faced many dangers on their journey. One night, bandits stormed into their camp.
Bandits!
We're under attack!
Marco, get up.
What is it?
Quick, we have to get out of here!

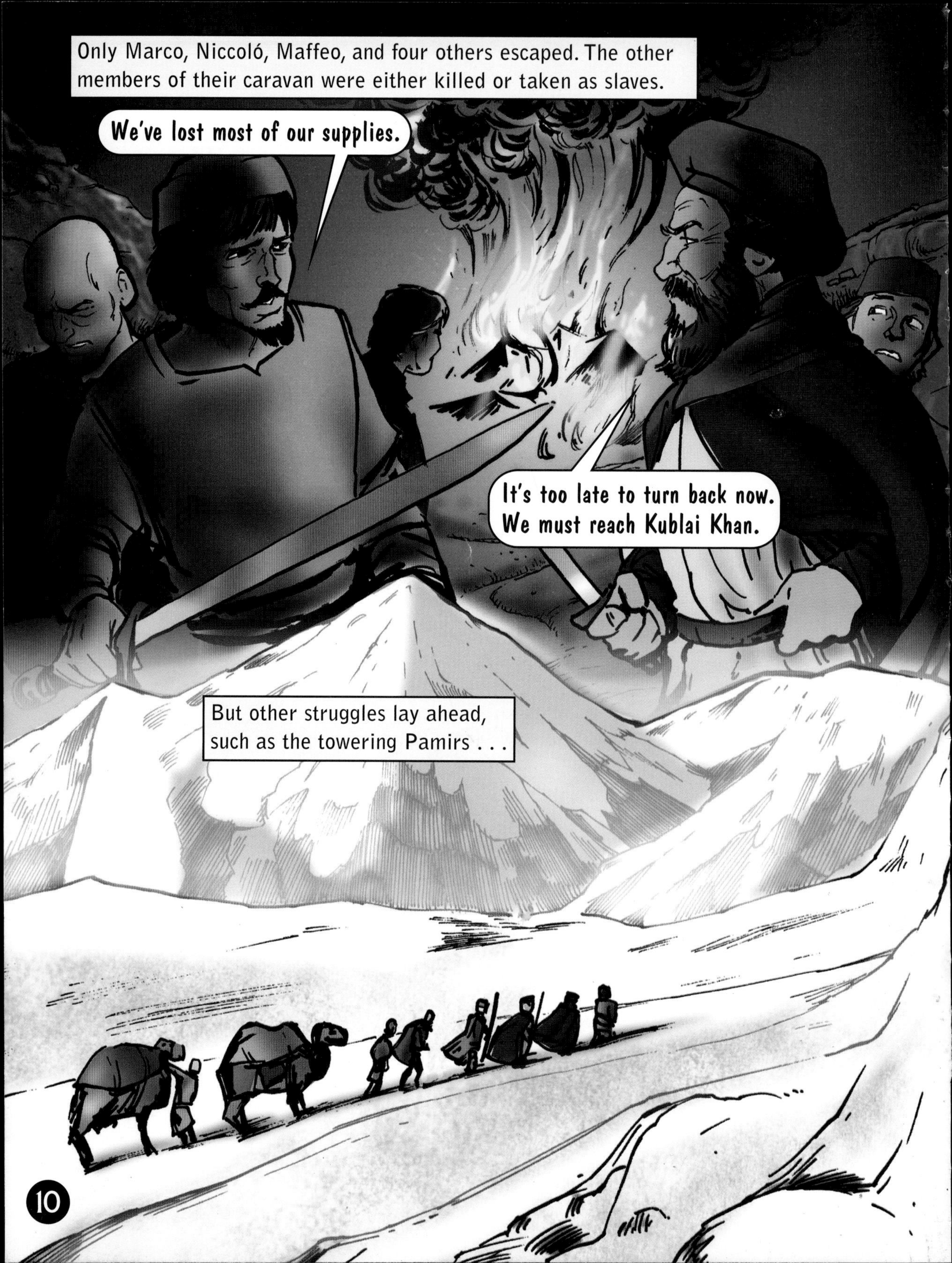

Only Marco, Niccoló, Maffeo, and four others escaped. The other members of their caravan were either killed or taken as slaves.
We've lost most of our supplies.
It's too late to turn back now. We must reach Kublai Khan.
But other struggles lay ahead, such as the towering Pamirs . . .

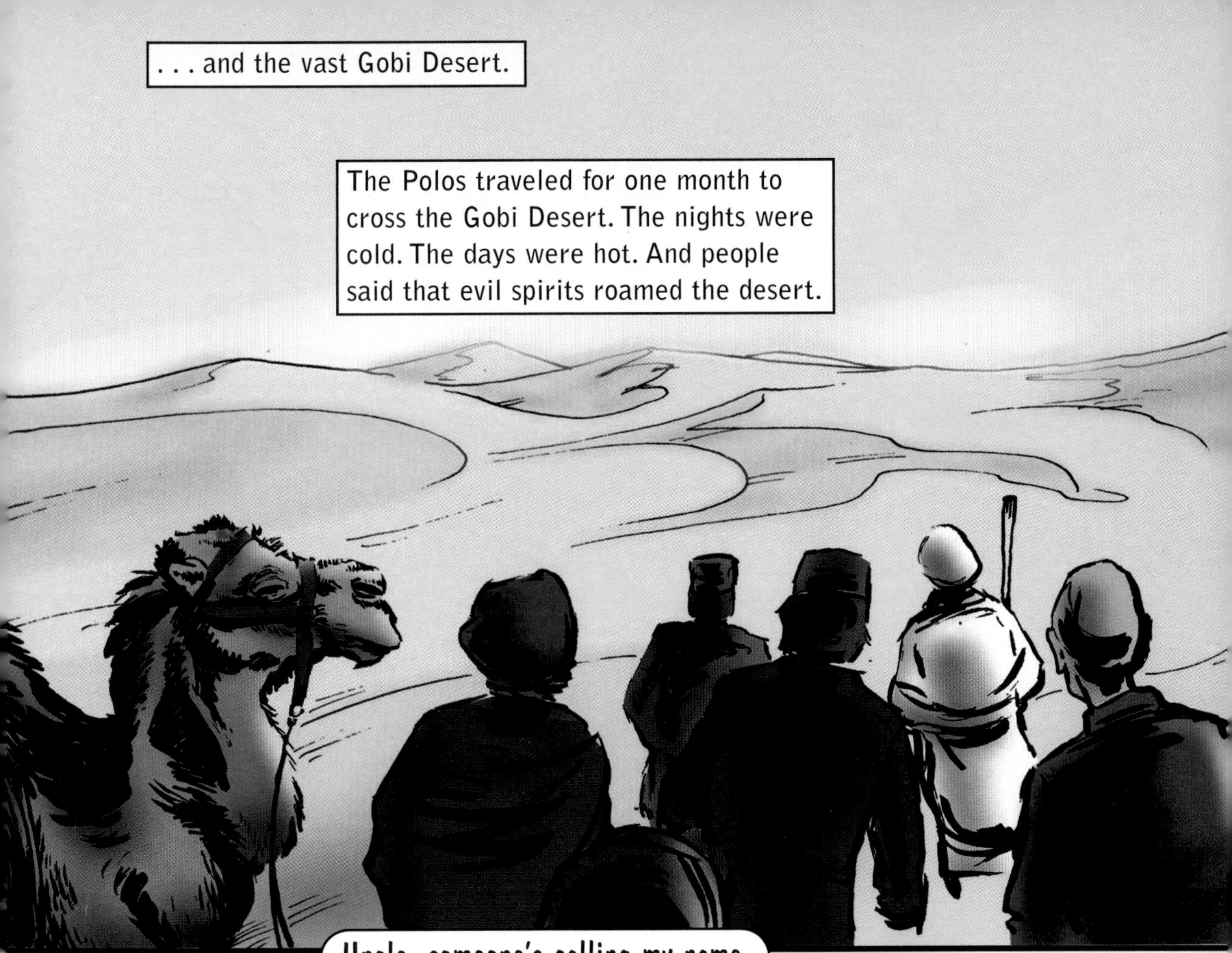
. . . and the vast Gobi Desert.
The Polos traveled for one month to cross the Gobi Desert. The nights were cold. The days were hot. And people said that evil spirits roamed the desert.

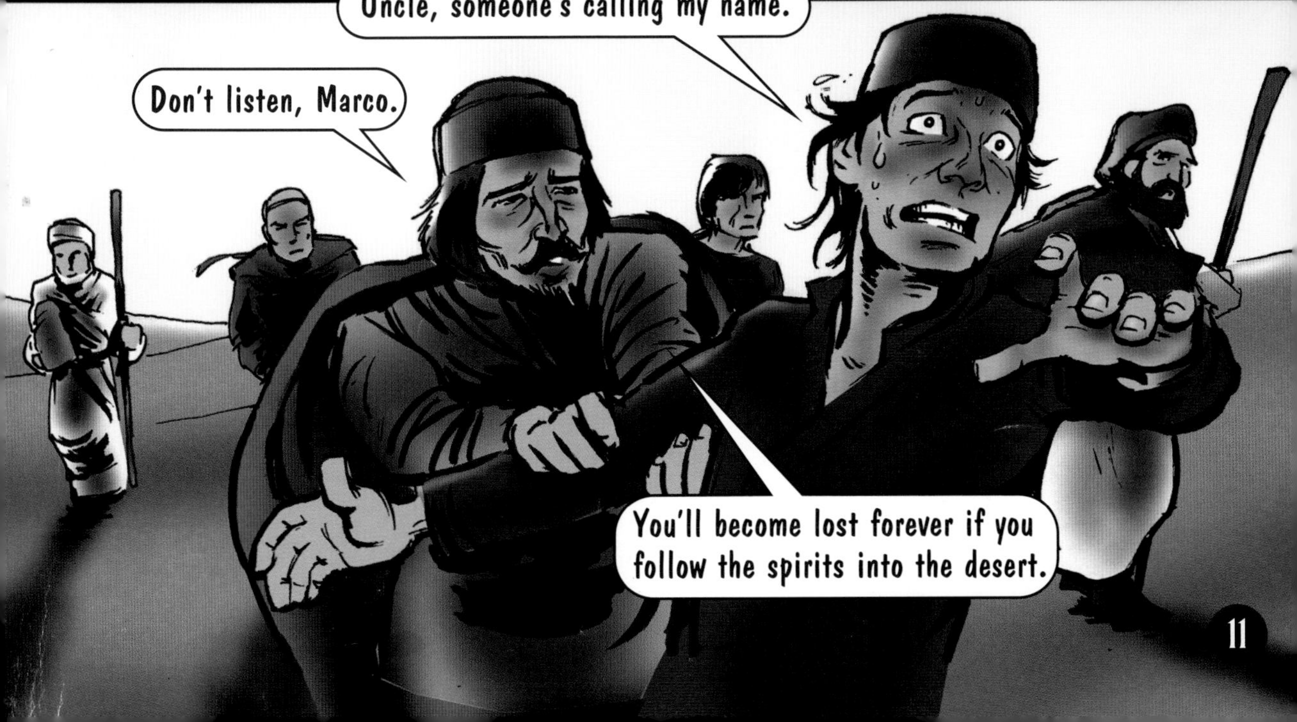
Uncle, someone's calling my name.
Don't listen, Marco.
You'll become lost forever if you follow the spirits into the desert.

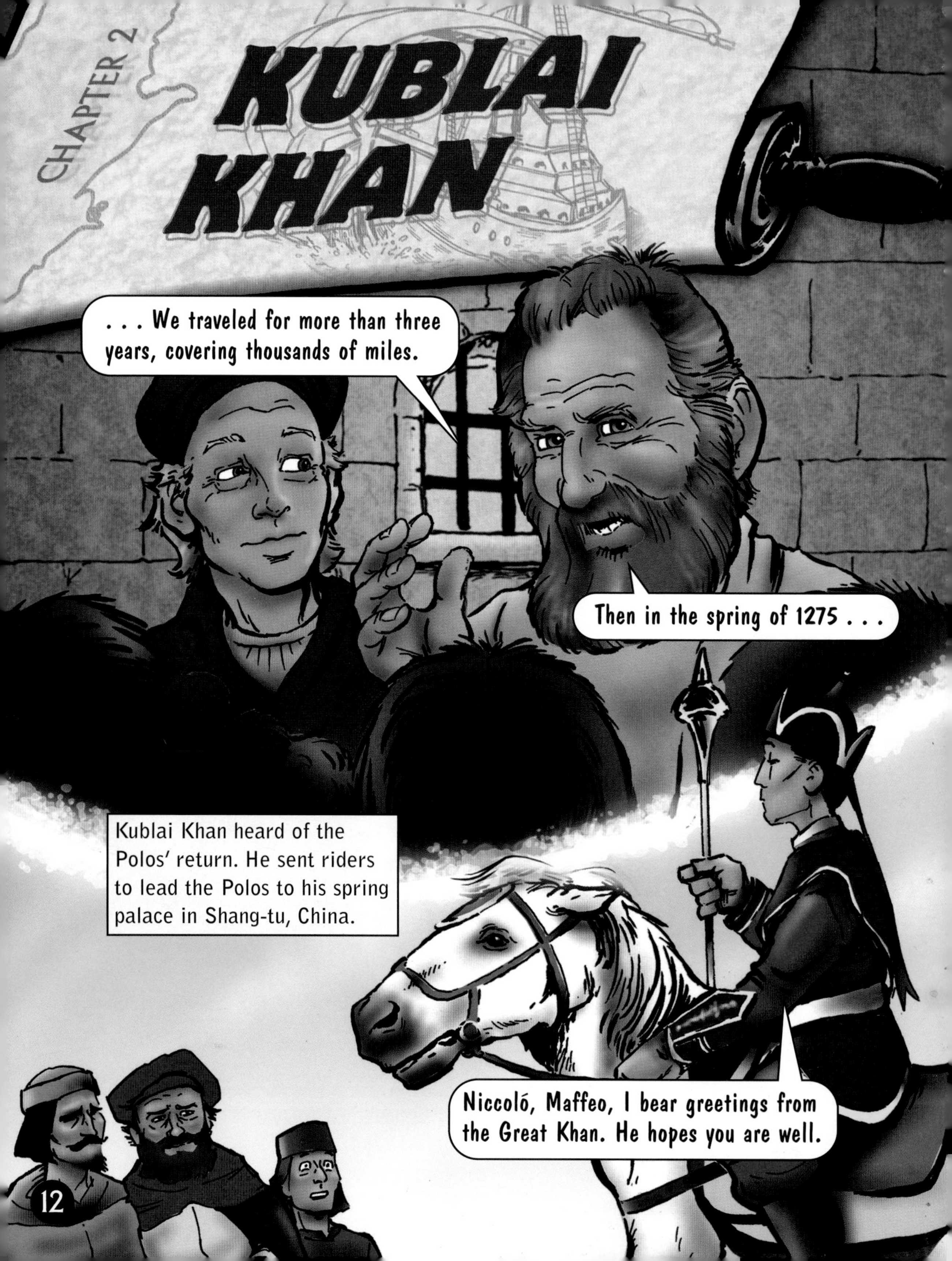
CHAPTER 2
KUBLAI KHAN
. . . We traveled for more than three years, covering thousands of miles.
Then in the spring of 1275 . . .
Kublai Khan heard of the Polos' return. He sent riders to lead the Polos to his spring palace in Shang-tu, China.
Niccoló, Maffeo, I bear greetings from the Great Khan. He hopes you are well.

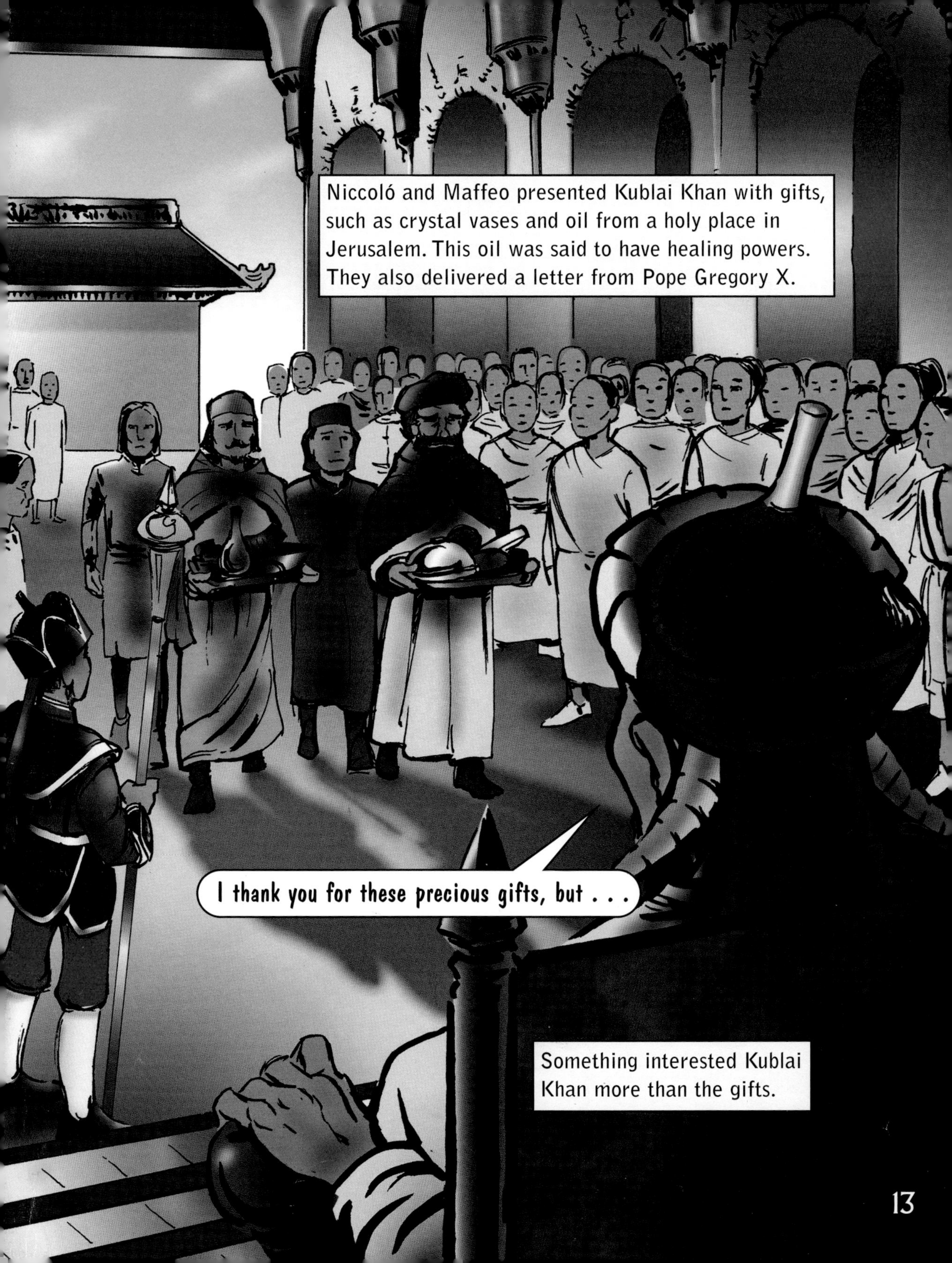

Niccoló and Maffeo presented Kublai Khan with gifts, such as crystal vases and oil from a holy place in Jerusalem. This oil was said to have healing powers. They also delivered a letter from Pope Gregory X.
I thank you for these precious gifts, but . . .
Something interested Kublai Khan more than the gifts.

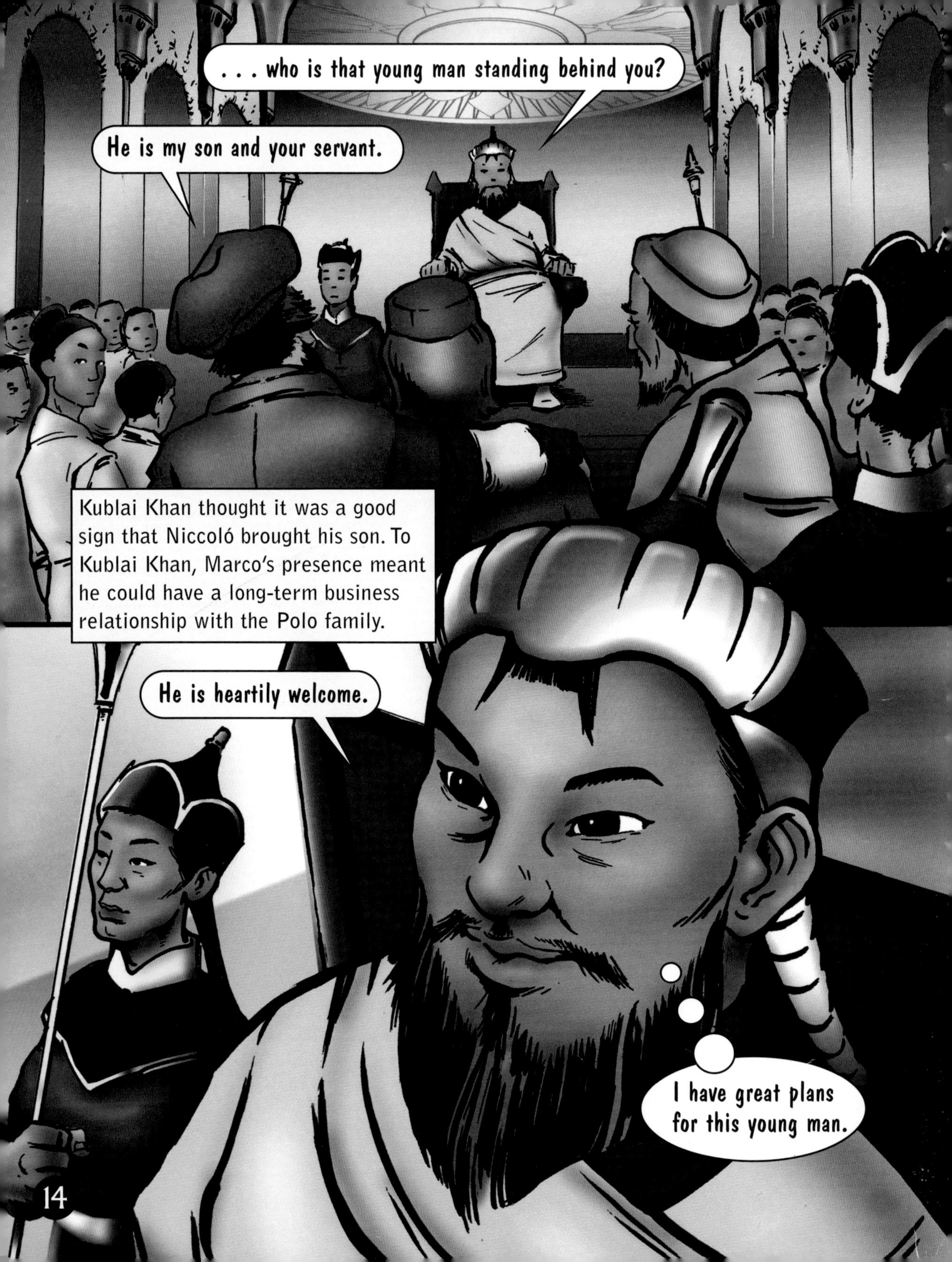

. . . who is that young man standing behind you?
He is my son and your servant.
Kublai Khan thought it was a good sign that Niccoló brought his son. To Kublai Khan, Marco's presence meant he could have a long-term business relationship with the Polo family.
He is heartily welcome.
I have great plans for this young man.

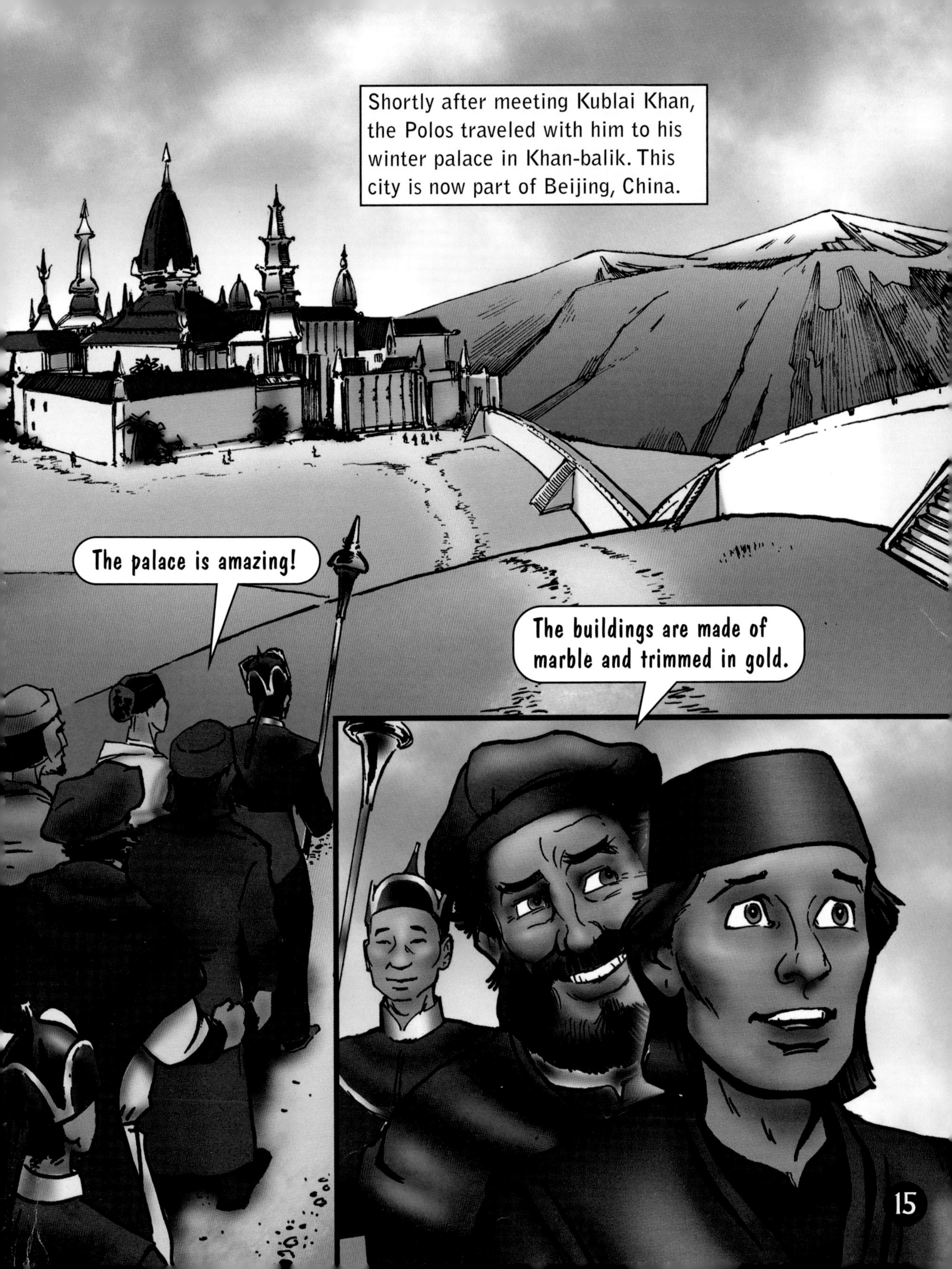
Shortly after meeting Kublai Khan, the Polos traveled with him to his winter palace in Khan-balik. This city is now part of Beijing, China.
The palace is amazing!
The buildings are made of marble and trimmed in gold.

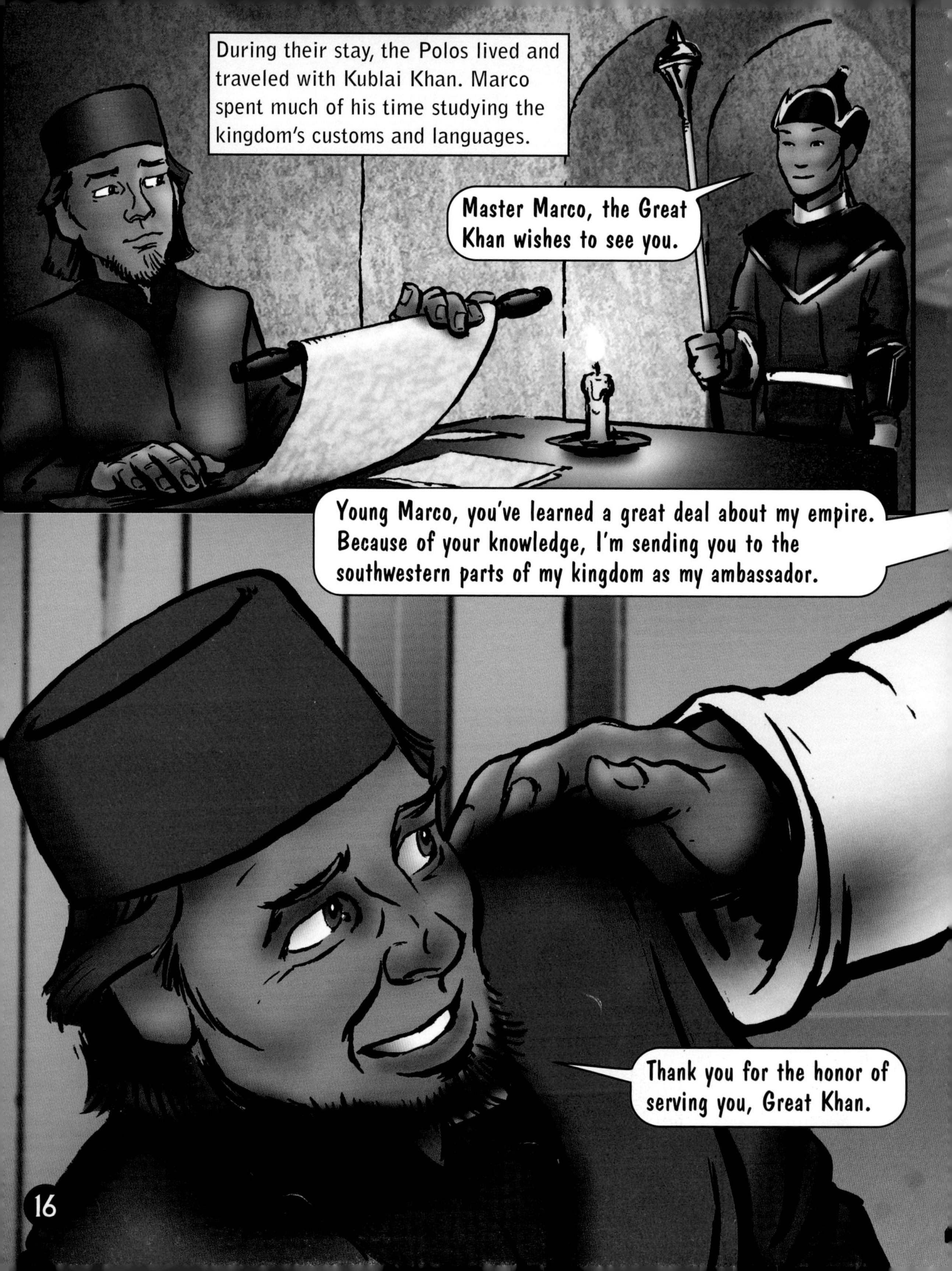
During their stay, the Polos lived and traveled with Kublai Khan. Marco spent much of his time studying the kingdom's customs and languages.
Master Marco, the Great Khan wishes to see you.
Young Marco, you've learned a great deal about my empire. Because of your knowledge, I'm sending you to the southwestern parts of my kingdom as my ambassador.
Thank you for the honor of serving you, Great Khan.

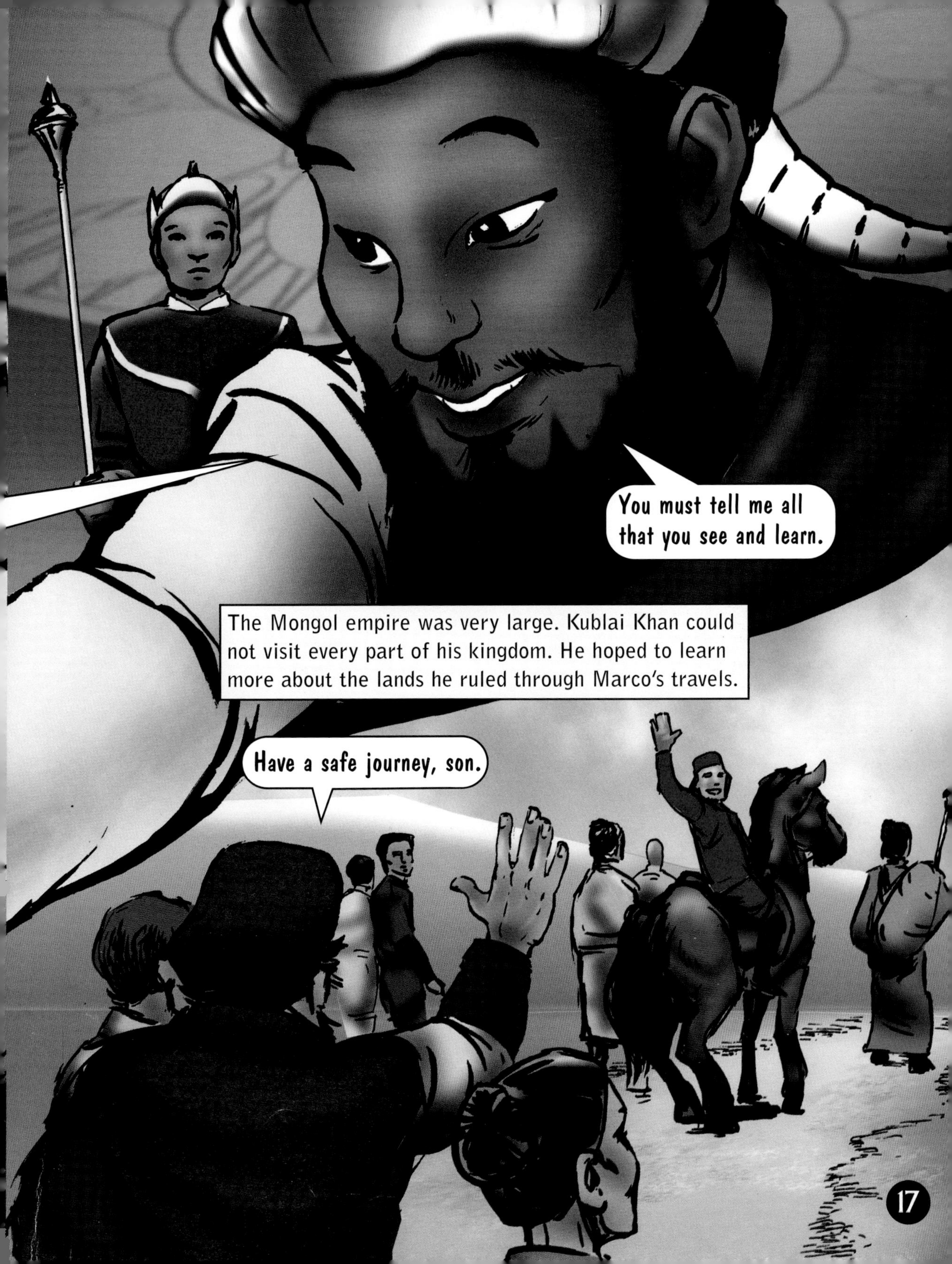
You must tell me all that you see and learn.
The Mongol empire was very large. Kublai Khan could not visit every part of his kingdom. He hoped to learn more about the lands he ruled through Marco's travels.
Have a safe journey, son.

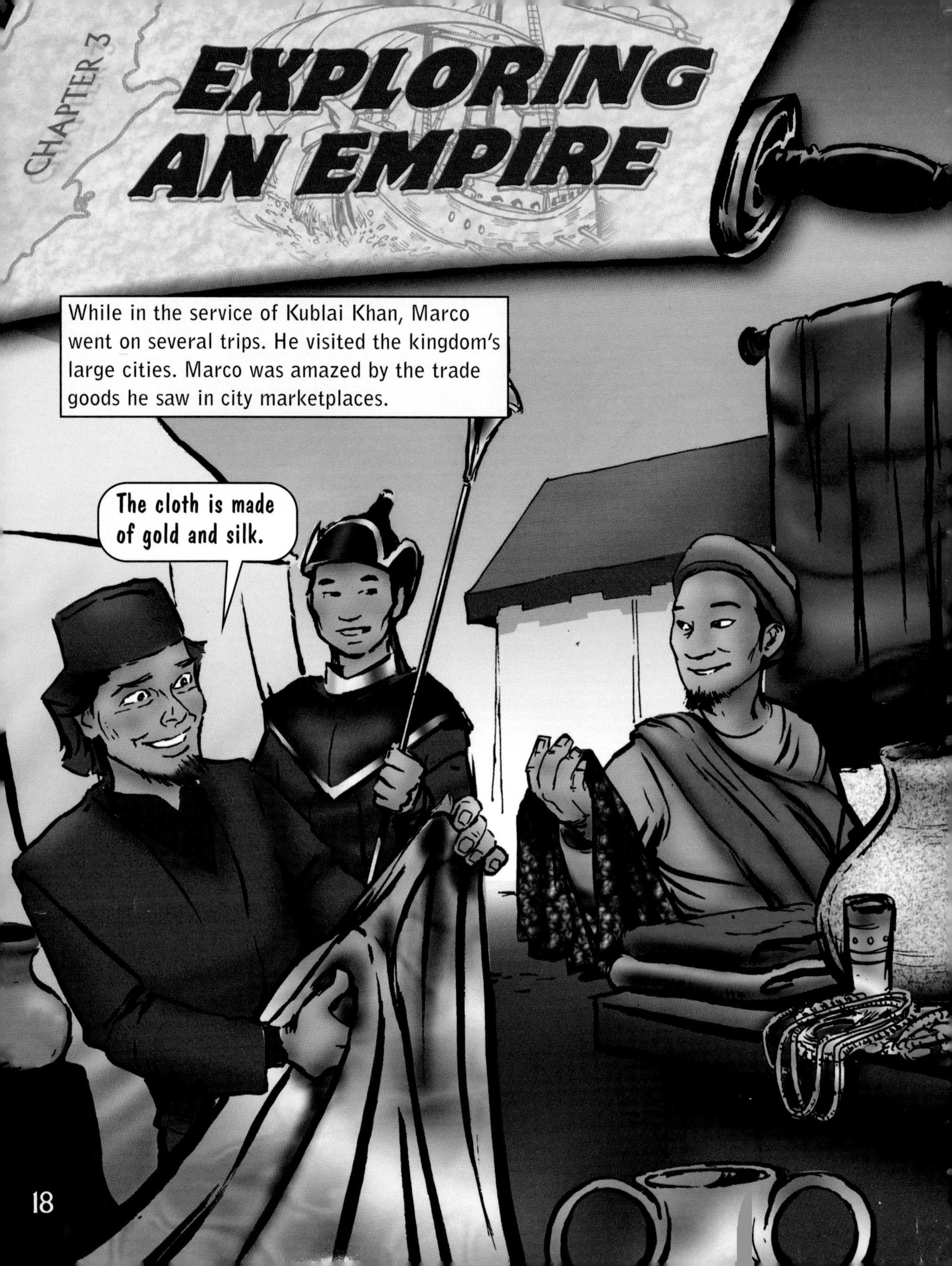
CHAPTER 3
EXPLORING AN EMPIRE
While in the service of Kublai Khan, Marco went on several trips. He visited the kingdom's large cities. Marco was amazed by the trade goods he saw in city marketplaces.
The cloth is made of gold and silk.

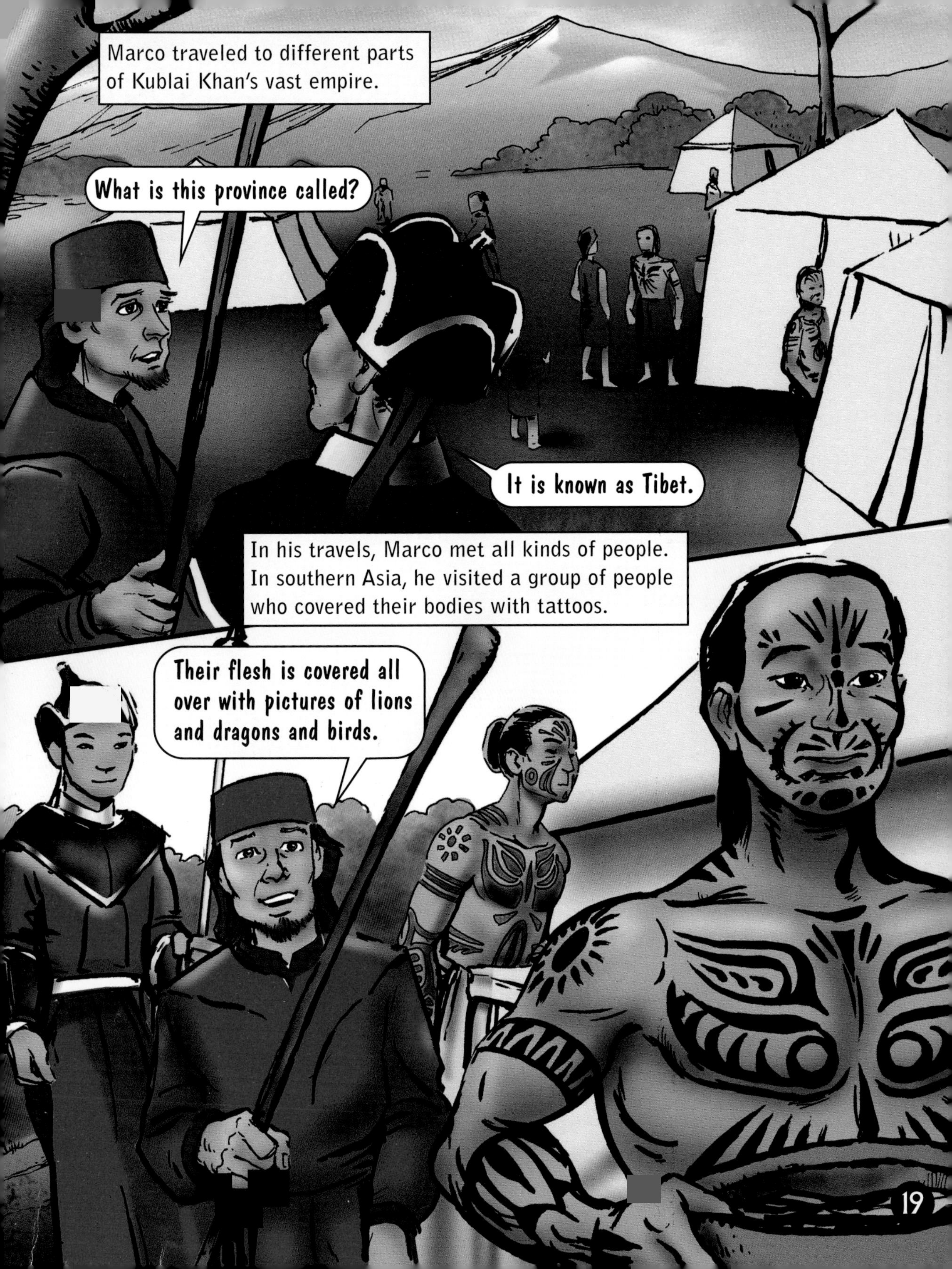
Marco traveled to different parts of Kublai Khan's vast empire.
What is this province called?
It is known as Tibet.
In his travels, Marco met all kinds of people. In southern Asia, he visited a group of people who covered their bodies with tattoos.
Their flesh is covered all over with pictures of lions and dragons and birds.

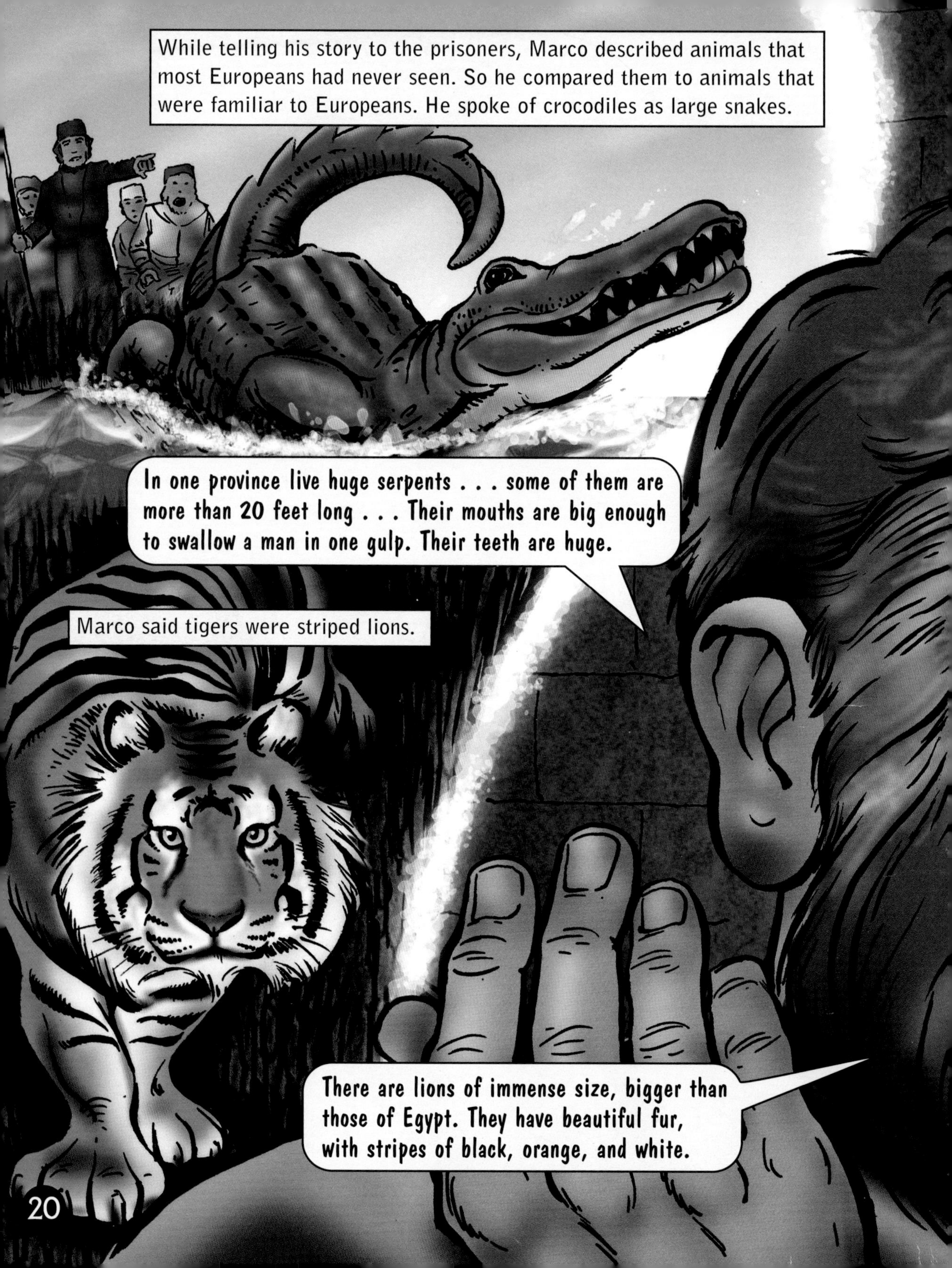
While telling his story to the prisoners, Marco described animals that most Europeans had never seen. So he compared them to animals that were familiar to Europeans. He spoke of crocodiles as large snakes.
In one province live huge serpents . . . some of them are more than 20 feet long . . . Their mouths are big enough to swallow a man in one gulp. Their teeth are huge.
Marco said tigers were striped lions.
There are lions of immense size, bigger than those of Egypt. They have beautiful fur, with stripes of black, orange, and white.

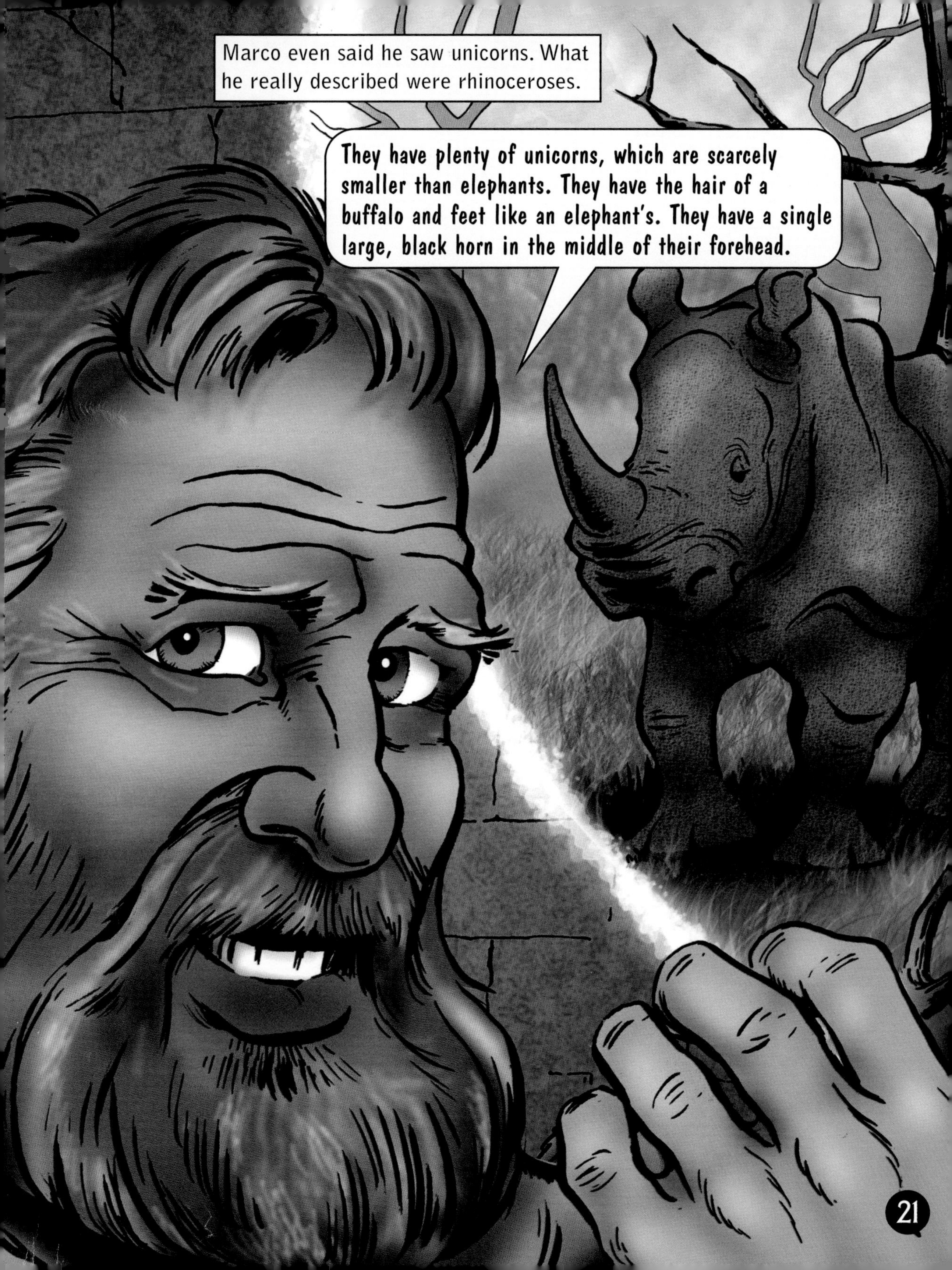
Marco even said he saw unicorns. What he really described were rhinoceroses.
They have plenty of unicorns, which are scarcely smaller than elephants. They have the hair of a buffalo and feet like an elephant's. They have a single large, black horn in the middle of their forehead.

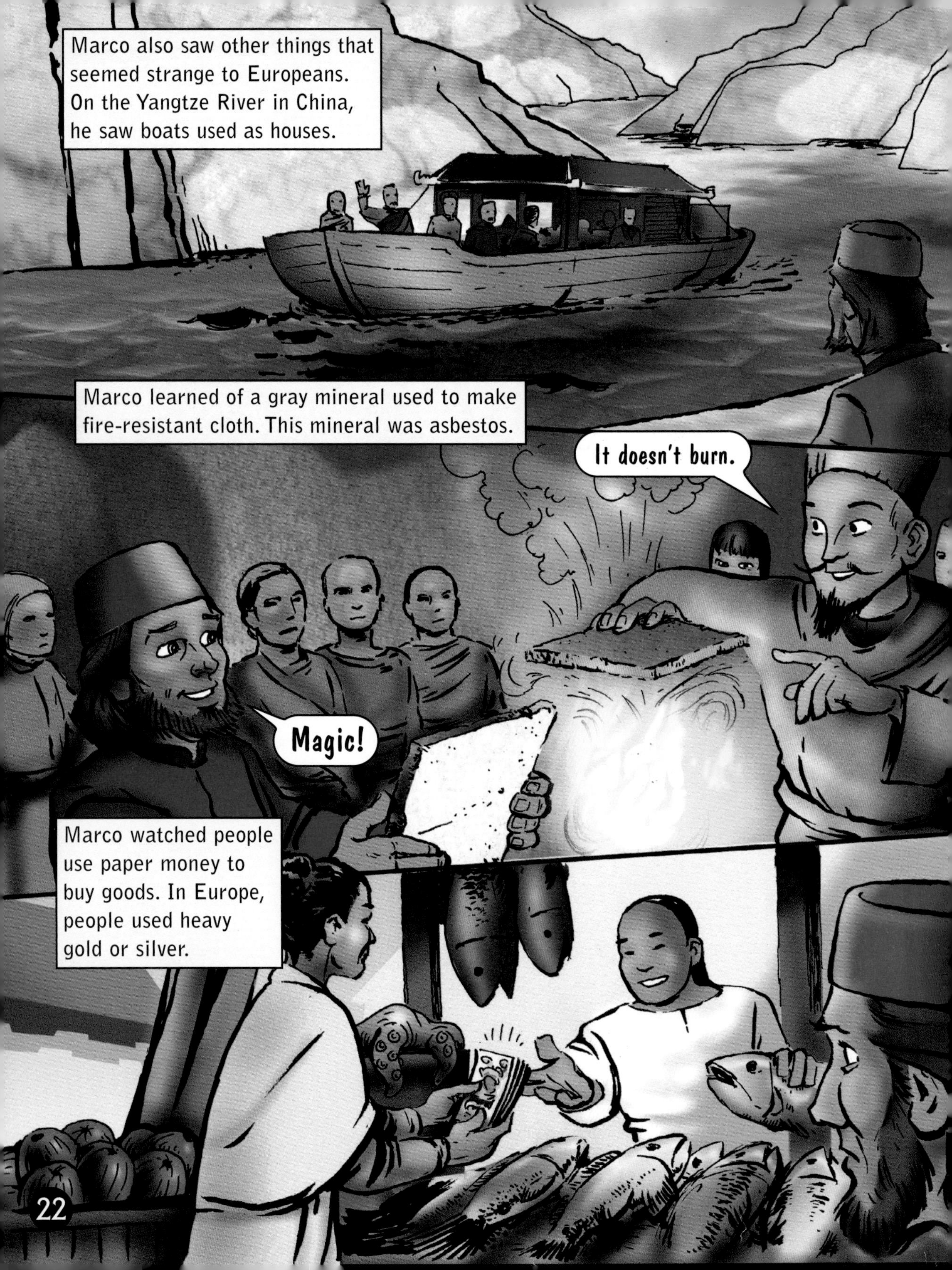
Marco also saw other things that seemed strange to Europeans. On the Yangtze River in China, he saw boats used as houses.
Marco learned of a gray mineral used to make fire-resistant cloth. This mineral was asbestos.
It doesn't burn.
Magic!
Marco watched people use paper money to buy goods. In Europe, people used heavy gold or silver.

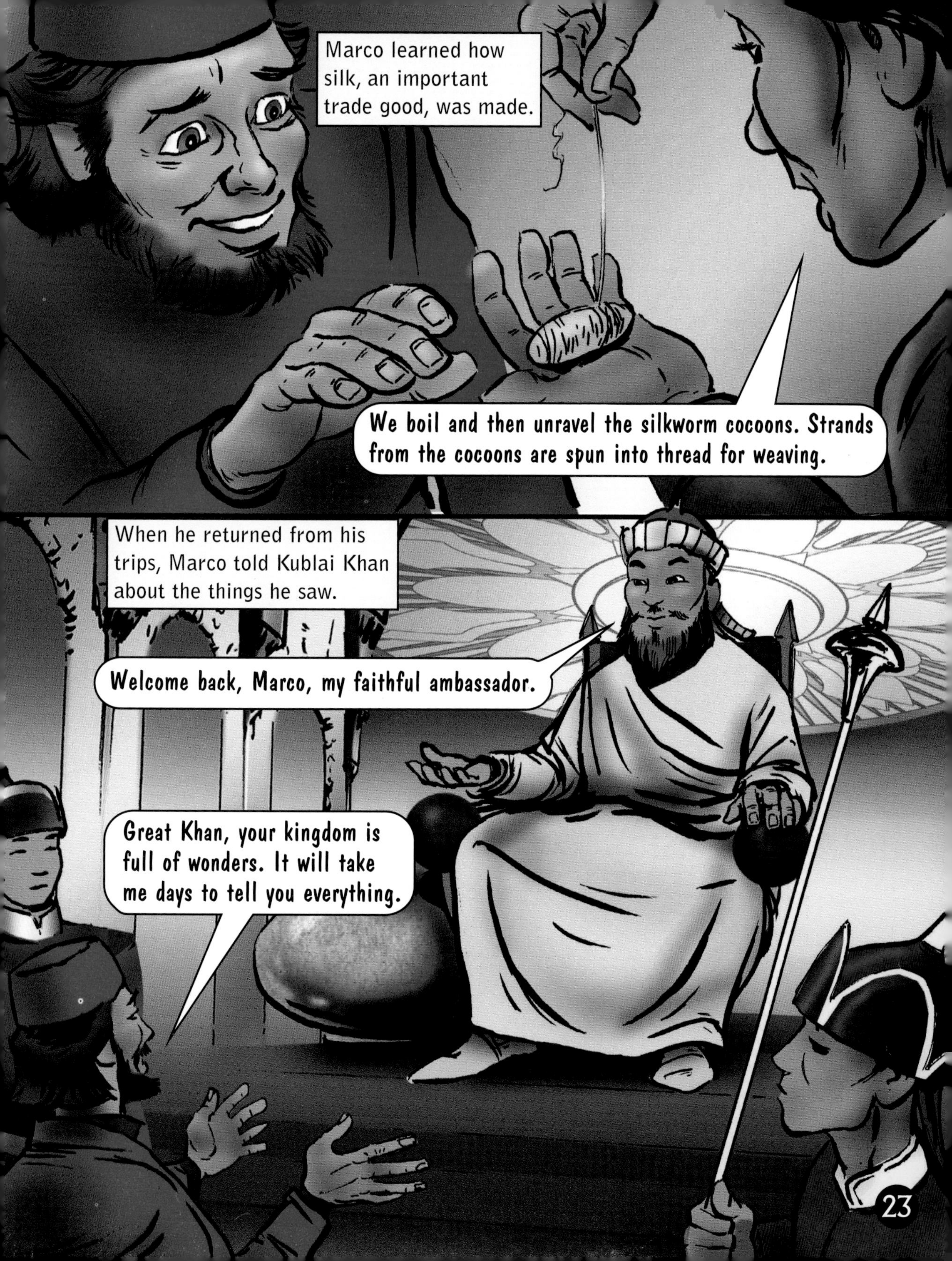

Marco learned how silk, an important trade good, was made.
We boil and then unravel the silkworm cocoons. Strands from the cocoons are spun into thread for weaving.
When he returned from his trips, Marco told Kublai Khan about the things he saw.
Welcome back, Marco, my faithful ambassador.
Great Khan, your kingdom is full of wonders. It will take me days to tell you everything.

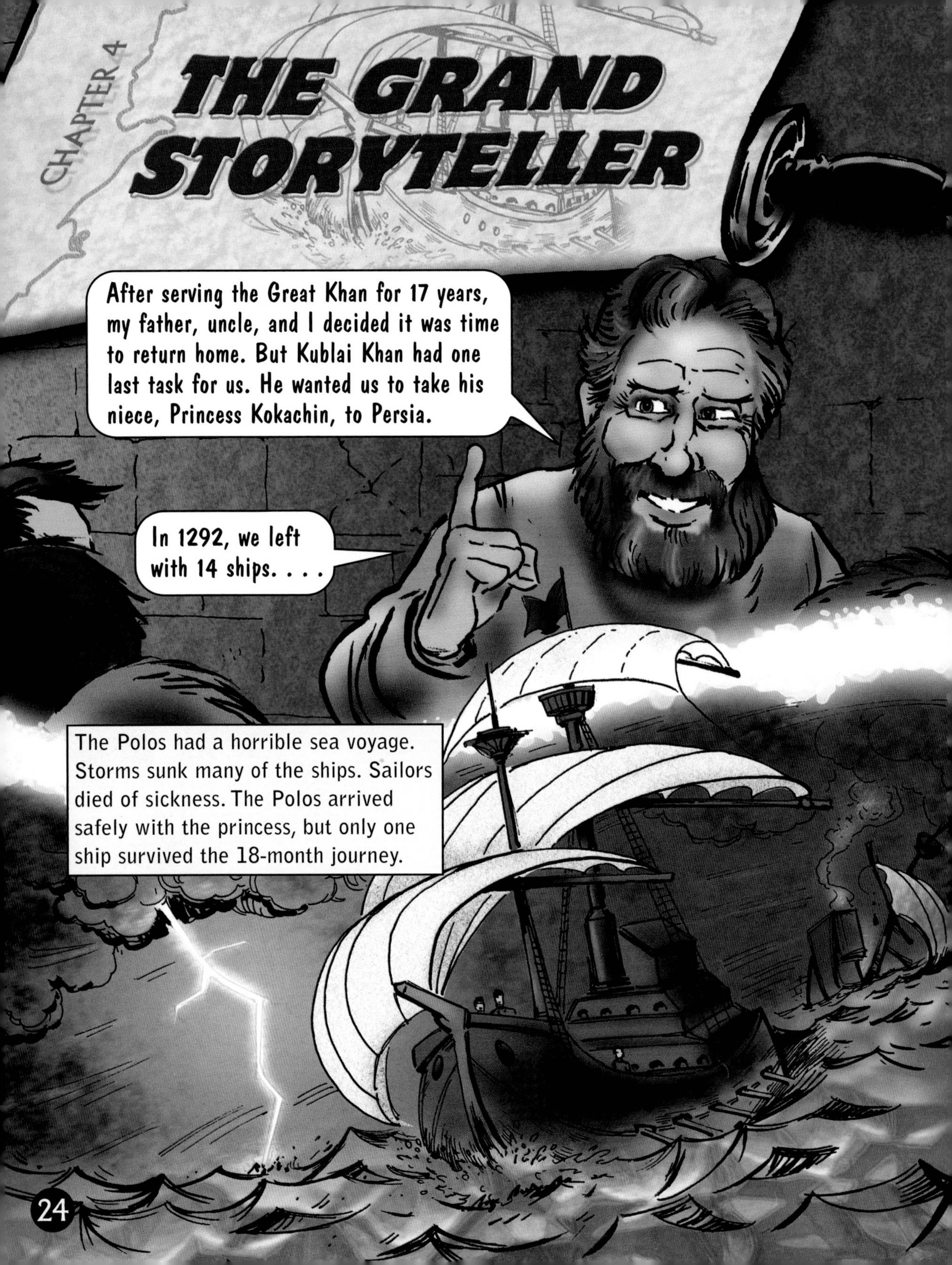
CHAPTER 4
THE GRAND STORYTELLER
After serving the Great Khan for 17 years, my father, uncle, and I decided it was time to return home. But Kublai Khan had one last task for us. He wanted us to take his niece, Princess Kokachin, to Persia.
In 1292, we left with 14 ships. . . .
The Polos had a horrible sea voyage. Storms sunk many of the ships. Sailors died of sickness. The Polos arrived safely with the princess, but only one ship survived the 18-month journey.

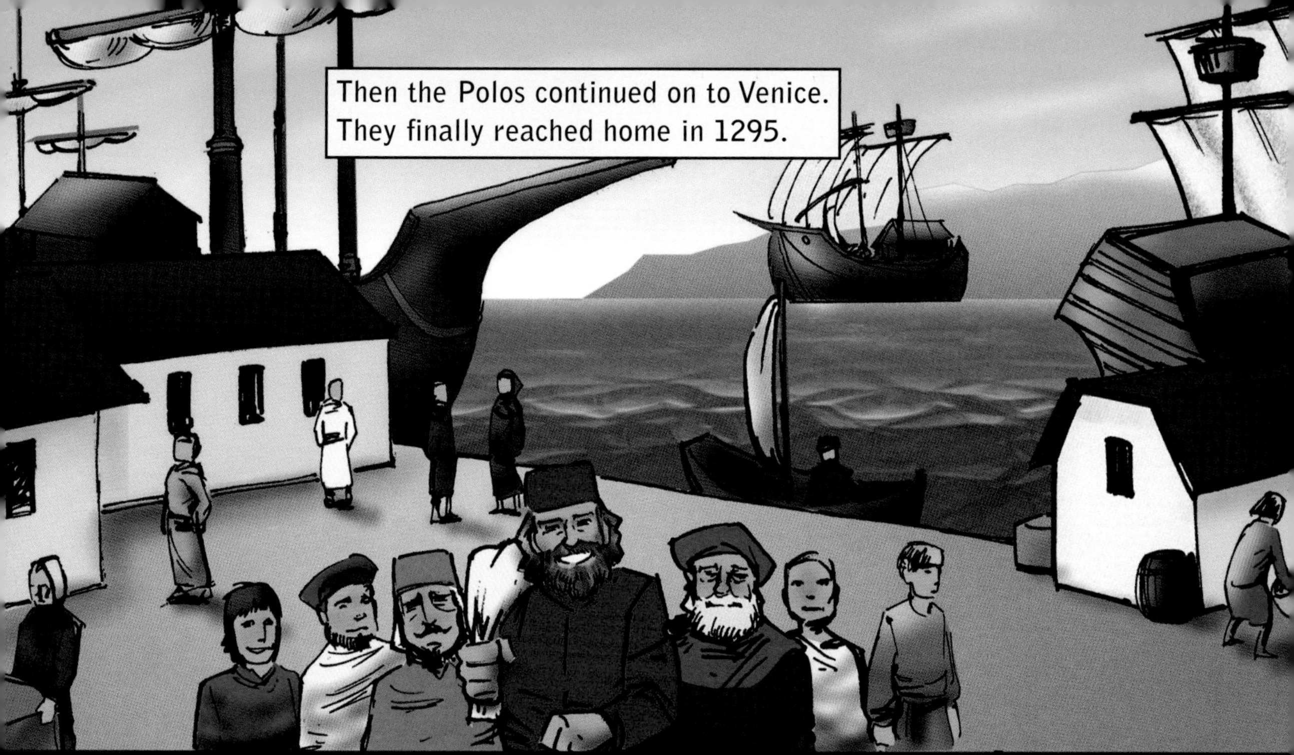
Then the Polos continued on to Venice. They finally reached home in 1295.

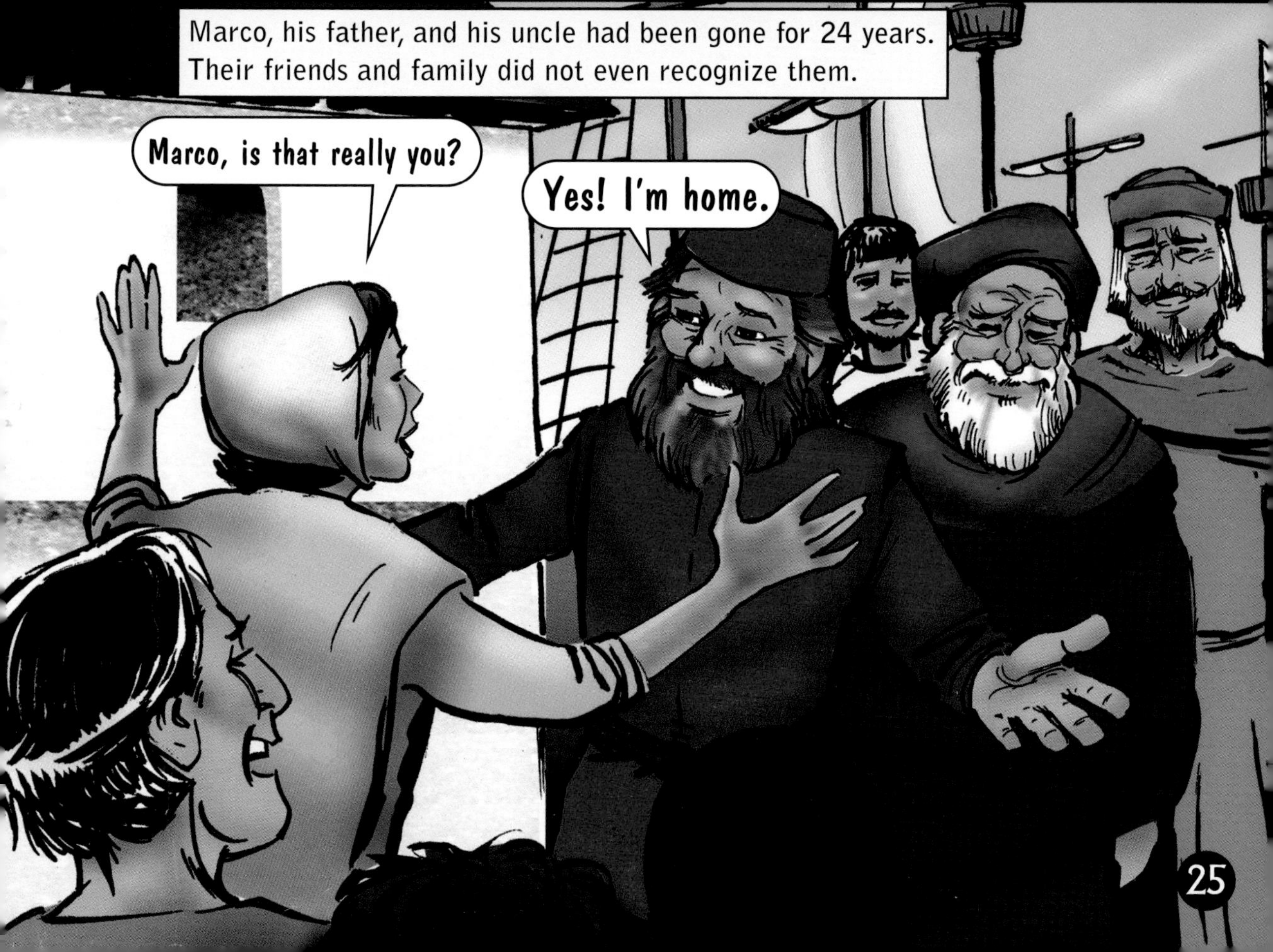
Marco, his father, and his uncle had been gone for 24 years. Their friends and family did not even recognize them.
Marco, is that really you?
Yes! I'm home.

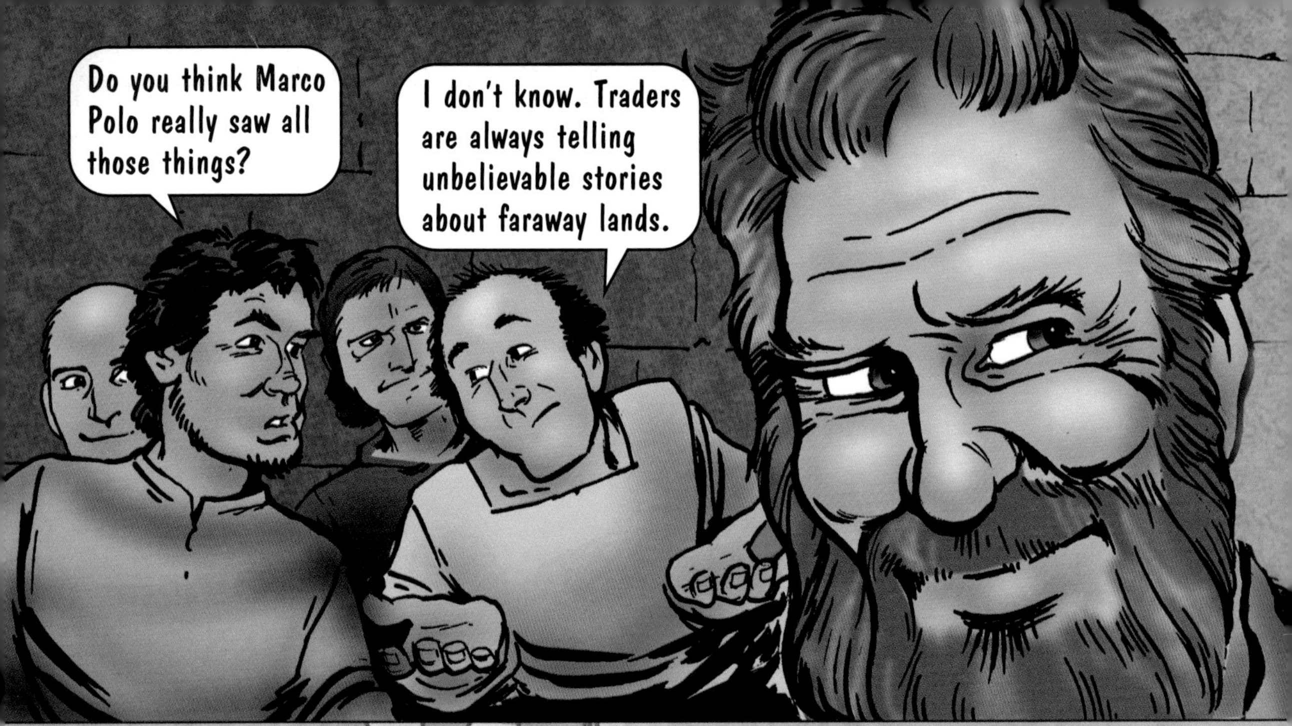
Do you think Marco Polo really saw all those things?
I don't know. Traders are always telling unbelievable stories about faraway lands.

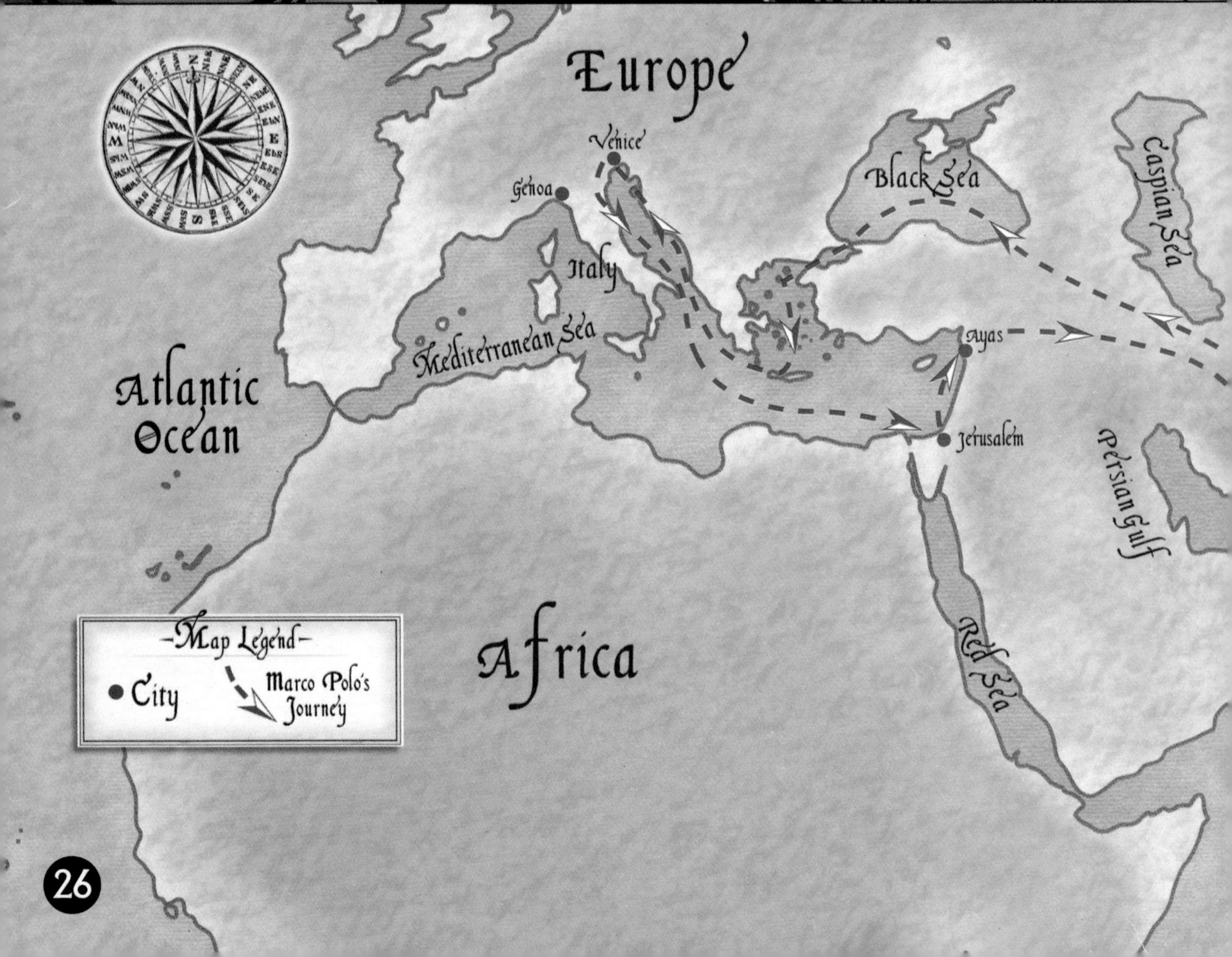
Europe
Venice
Genoa
Italy
Black Sea
Caspian Sea
Mediterranean Sea
Ayas
Atlantic Ocean
Jerusalem
Persian Gulf
Red Sea
Africa
Map Legend
City
Marco Polo's Journey

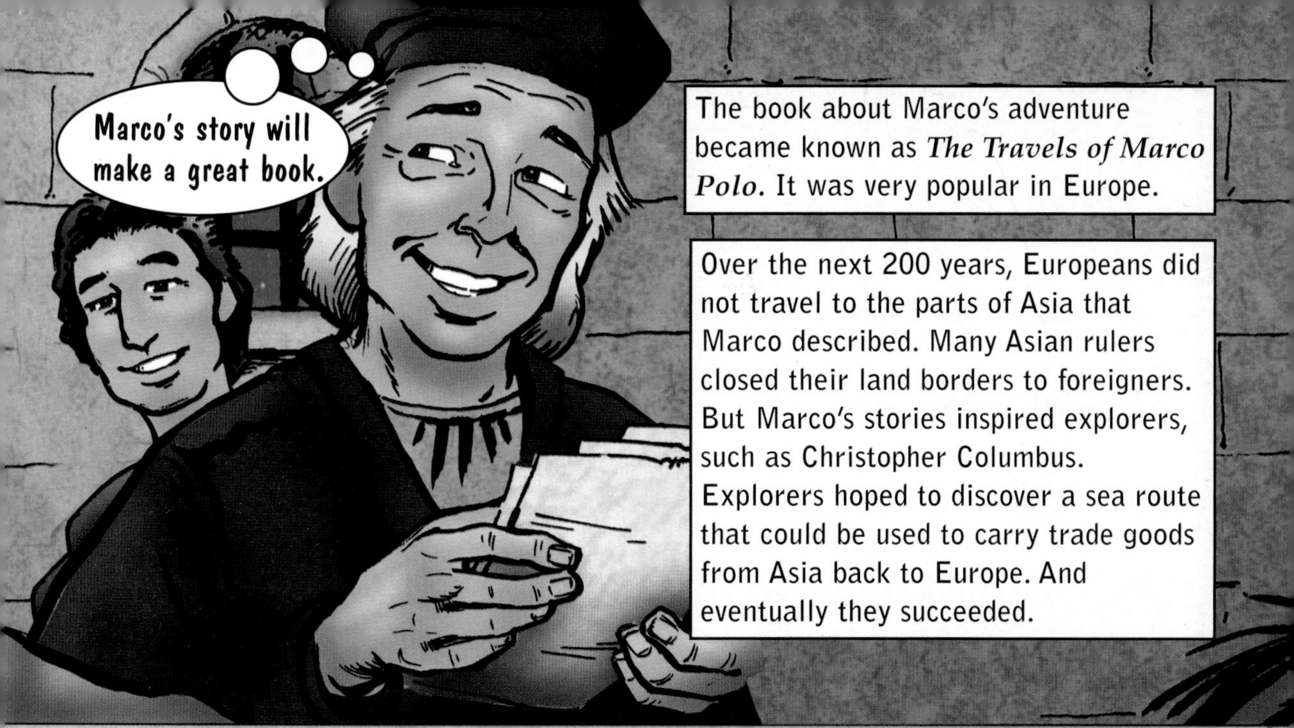
Marco's story will make a great book.
The book about Marco's adventure became known as *The Travels of Marco Polo.* It was very popular in Europe.
Over the next 200 years, Europeans did not travel to the parts of Asia that Marco described. Many Asian rulers closed their land borders to foreigners. But Marco's stories inspired explorers, such as Christopher Columbus. Explorers hoped to discover a sea route that could be used to carry trade goods from Asia back to Europe. And eventually they succeeded.

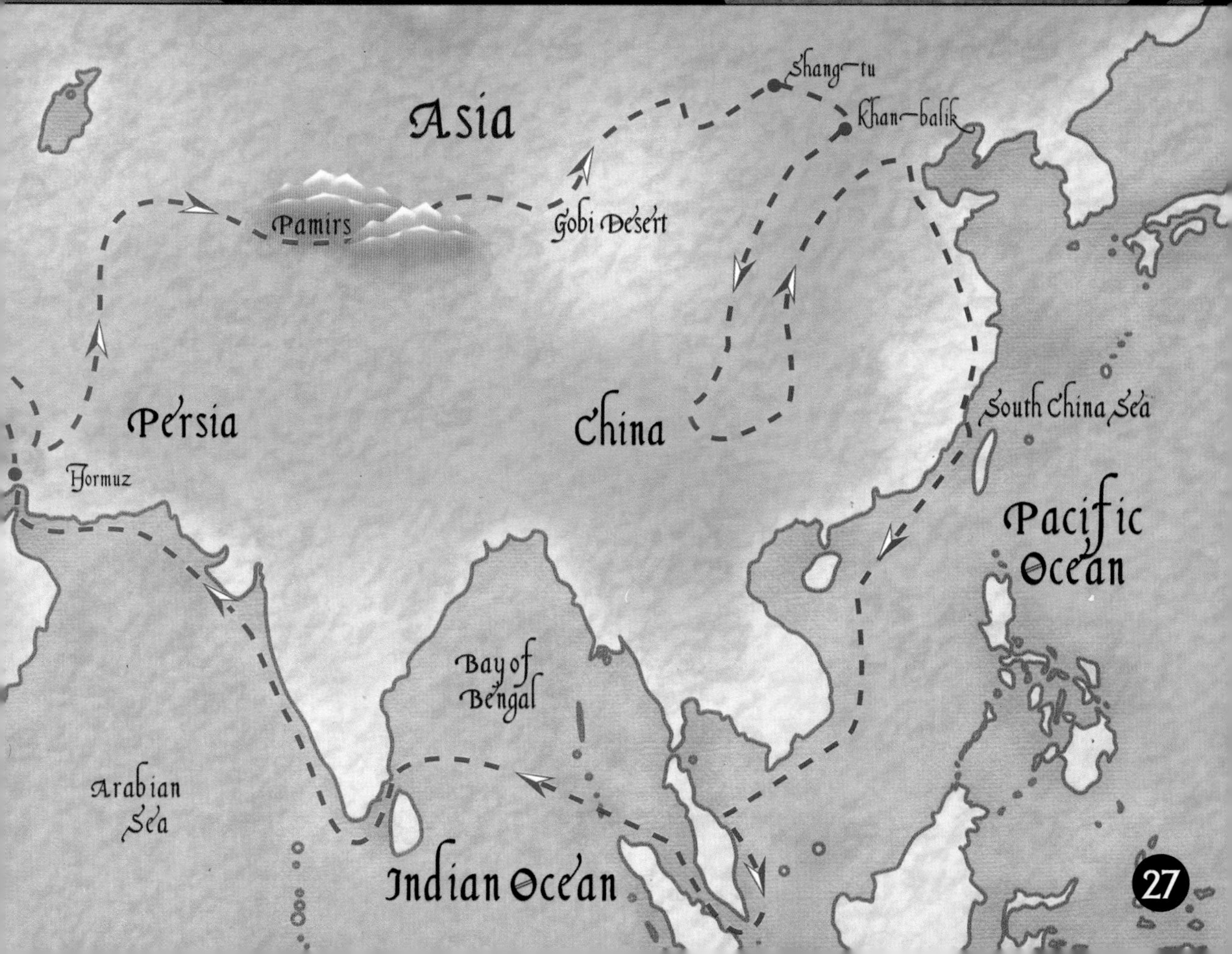
Shang-tu
Asia
Khan-balik
Pamirs
Gobi Desert
Persia
China
South China Sea
Hormuz
Pacific Ocean
Bay of Bengal
Arabian Sea
Indian Ocean

More about Marco Polo

- Marco Polo was born in 1254 on the island of Korcula. This island was ruled by the city of Venice at the time. It is now part of Croatia.

- Marco's mother died while Niccoló and Maffeo were on their first trip to China. Marco was raised by his aunt.

- Marco did not really hear evil spirits while traveling through the Gobi Desert. The sounds people heard were created by wind blowing through desert plants and trees.

- Genoa and Venice fought four wars to gain control of trade routes in the Mediterranean Sea. Marco fought in the second war, which lasted from 1293 to 1299.

- Marco was taken prisoner on September 6, 1298, in a sea battle near the island of Korcula. The Venetians lost almost all of their ships, and about 14,000 sailors were either killed or captured during the battle.

- Marco was released from prison in 1299. He died in 1324 in Venice.

- Kublai Khan asked the Polos to bring him 100 religious men who could teach him about Christianity. Only two such men agreed to join the Polos. But they quickly grew afraid during the long, dangerous journey to China and returned home.

- Kublai Khan was the grandson of the great Mongol leader Genghis Khan. The Mongol Empire created by Genghis Khan was the largest land empire in history. At one time, the Mongols ruled nearly all of the land from Korea and China to eastern Europe.

- Many historians do not believe that Marco Polo ever went to China. They point out that Marco did not mention the Great Wall of China, an important landmark. Historians say that what is really important is the way in which *The Travels of Marco Polo* affected people in Europe. Marco's book inspired people to learn more about China and to find a sea route to Asia. In searching for a sea route, explorers learned about parts of the world that were unknown to Europeans.

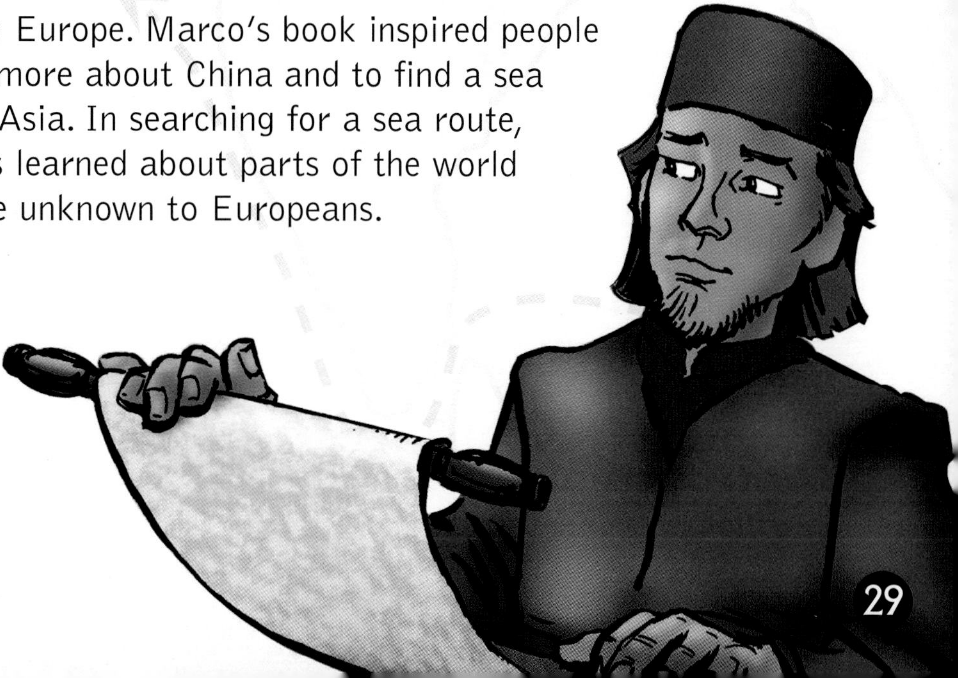

GLOSSARY

ambassador (am-BASS-uh-dur)—a person who represents a government in another country

asbestos (ass-BESS-tuhss)—a grayish mineral whose fibers can be woven into fireproof fabric

caravan (KAR-uh-van)—a group of people traveling together

custom (KUHSS-tuhm)—a tradition among a group of people

province (PRAW-vuhnss)—a district or region of some countries

tattoo (ta-TOO)—a picture that has been printed onto someone's skin with ink and needles

INTERNET SITES

FactHound offers a safe, fun way to find Internet sites related to this book. All of the sites on FactHound have been researched by our staff.

Here's how:

1. *Visit www.facthound.com*
2. Type in this special code **0736838309** for age-appropriate sites. Or enter a search word related to this book for a more general search.
3. Click on the **Fetch It** button.

FactHound will fetch the best sites for you!

READ MORE

Burgan, Michael. *Marco Polo: Marco Polo and the Silk Road to China.* Exploring the World. Minneapolis: Compass Point Books, 2002.

Deady, Kathleen W., and Muriel L. Dubois. *Ancient China.* Early Civilizations. Mankato, Minn.: Capstone Press, 2004.

Deedrick, Tami. *China.* Ancient Civilizations. Austin, Texas: Steadwell Books, 2001.

Zannos, Susan. *The Life and Times of Marco Polo.* Biography of Ancient Civilizations. Hockessin, Del.: Mitchell Lane Publishers, 2004.

BIBLIOGRAPHY

Fisher, Richard B. *The Marco Polo Expedition: A Journey along the Silk Road.* London: Hodder and Stoughton, 1988.

Polo, Marco. *The Travels of Marco Polo.* Translated by Ronald Latham. New York: Penguin Books, 1988.

Rossabi, Morris. *Khubilai Khan: His Life and Times.* Berkeley: University of California Press, 1988.

Wood, Frances. *Did Marco Polo Go to China?* London: Secker & Warburg, 1995.

INDEX